A FASCINATION FOR FEATHERS

Book design, illustrations, and photographs by Connie M. Thompson, unless otherwise credited. Manufactured and written in the United States of America.

Published by **Ridge Road Enterprises**
14488 S. Ridge Road, Dafter, MI 49724
www.ridgeroadenter.com
Email: bbirder@hughes.net

First Edition

ISBN 978-0-578-08357-5

Library of Congress Control Number 2011907328

Printed in the United States of America

These stories are written from memory and represent true events as best as the writer can recollect. They are not meant to defame or offend anyone.

In memory of Jake -
You'll always be in my heart

A Fascination for Feathers

Observations, tales, and recollections about birds

Connie M. Thompson

With contributions, insight, and input from the wonderful people of the Eastern Upper Peninsula of Michigan

DEDICATION:

To my husband, Pat,
My best friend and lover,
My staunchest supporter and
Unwavering believer.
Through thick and thin
I'll always be at your side,
When I said 'I do,'
I meant 'Hang on for the ride!'

To my good friends, Tom & Carley Ball,
for your inspiration and your continual support in
everything that I do.

To my beautiful friend, Vicki Manfrin,
whose continual smile and uplifting Christian attitude give me the
courage to feel that anything is possible.

Special thanks to Joe Nault,
for sharing great bird sightings with us over the years.

FOREWORD

This is not a book like most other books about birds. Most birding books are written by people who have spent their whole lives pursuing birds in one fashion or another, or by others that hold down jobs at nature centers, wildlife observatories, refuges, or the like - in other words, they are written by bird professionals.

The difference here is that I have not always been a bird-lover. Not that I hated birds, mind you, I just never took notice of them for over thirty years. Oh sure, I knew what chickadees, cardinals, and goldfinches were and I could usually pick out a seagull or a crow, but throw a warbler at me and I was simply lost.

I lived my life like most other hard-working folks, held down a job or two at a time, and had fun with my friends and family when I could. We went to the beach, to the woods, hiked along trails, rode bicycles along roadsides, had picnics, and played frisbee in the parks. The birds were all around me during those times, often right beside me, but I was just too distracted to pay attention. I was busy doing what most other people did, lived my life, and paid attention only to my immediate surroundings.

What changed all that for me? Even though I had been a nature enthusiast all my life, it was not a part of wage-earning, so it always played "second fiddle," you might say, in my free time.

As I think back to my upbringing, I remember that my mother always had a bird book nearby and that she had an interest in birds, although it was never something that we discussed or even mentioned. And when I visited my grandparents' house, Grandpa Newman always had a pair of binoculars sitting on his desk in his study and a bird identification book was laying on a table close at hand. He also had a bird feeder right outside the living room window and sometimes when we went to their house the binoculars and the bird book would be on a TV tray right next to his easy chair. When I was tall enough to be able to see out the living room windows, I often saw many bright and colorful birds come in and out of the bird feeder. What drew my eye the most then - and today - was the bright and flashy cardinal in his suit of red with his black mask. When I got excited and pointed it out to Grandpa, his reaction was to show me what the cardinal looked like in his bird book and to point out to me what the female looked like too. And there was where my love of birds started. As I got older, boys and school and other items in life took over my interests and I totally forgot about birds.

Life changed for me when I took a new job in the Upper Peninsula of Michigan. I moved into a small house right in the middle of forty acres of wilderness, where nature and I got along or I didn't think I would survive. It was there I rediscovered my love of nature and all its creatures. I was awakened every morning by the blackbirds singing in the weeds surrounding the house and by the gulls and geese flying overhead on their way to the water's edge. Every morning the robins enthusiastically greeted the day in the nearby trees and every evening I fell asleep to the trilling chorus of many frogs' voices and the occasional soft hoot of a Canada goose on a neighbor's pond. When I heard the mournful cry of the loon as it flew into its nightly resting place, I knew I was hooked on my new lifestyle.

It was in this tiny home that I remembered what living in the country had been like when I was young, and how very much I had missed it after living in a big city for over twelve years. It was here that I found my fascination with birds again and how they led me on an incredible journey that continues yet today.

After five or six years of learning the countryside and the people, I began to share my bird sightings with other local people who were also interested in birds. This sharing of information led me to read a weekly bird column that a man named Warren Parker wrote for the local newspaper. His columns were informative and deepened my fascination for the birding world. Later, I became related to Warren when I married a local man. Warren often shared his birding insights with me and let me in on a few secrets now and then too. He was always generous with bird-lovers, was well-known for his bird knowledge and many people patronized his hardware store simply to get some of his bird advice on what type of feeder or bird house to buy. After years of writing for the newspaper, Warren's health took a turn for the worse and he decided to quit writing his column and pursue other interests.

I felt that this created a gap in our local community and I proposed that the newspaper let me continue in Warren's place. I would not be writing for him, or replacing him, but instead would try to offer the same type of incredible and interesting information that he had always provided. The newspaper agreed to let me try writing the column, and the ensuing response that the new column created overwhelmed us all.

I was enthusiastically welcomed by the community with open arms and the response continues even to this day. I dedicate this book to everyone who has ever shared with me their bird sightings, their questions about birds and, in general, their fascination with one of nature's most incredible creatures - birds.

For it has been the readers that made my newspaper column what it was in those days. After I quit working for the newspaper, I found that I still wanted to be involved with the incredible community of bird-lovers. So I continued to share what I learned every month with my newfound friends in a monthly newsletter called *Birds In Our Backyards* that I offered to whomever was interested.

I try to learn something about birds every month, and I share that knowledge with the readers just as they share their knowledge with me. They have taken me along on an amazing ride that has boggled my mind at times. This book is about what we have all learned on the journey together, from the plain to the almost supernatural sightings. The anecdotes and the bird-story sharing have been wonderful and I can't begin to tell everyone how much I have appreciated the calls, letters, e-mails, and even faxes! We have learned so much and shared so many experiences.

I do not now nor have I ever claimed to be any type of a bird "expert." I am more than willing to share what I do know and also am the first to admit when I don't know something!

That local man that I married - Pat - is the light of my life and he has been an incredible sport to travel this road with me. For over a decade he has been telling me to write a book - and now I have finally listened to him (did I mention how stubborn I am?). Pat has shared with me his own unique experiences from the "other side of the fence" you might say - the bird-hunting side. I would never have guessed that entwined with a love of hunting is also a love of the beauty of birds. He and I have learned alongside one another and shared many of these experiences. To this day I continue to rely on his knowledge of flying waterfowl - which continues to confound me.

The good Lord gave me a talent for writing and for being creative and I hope that He will continue to bless us as Pat and I pursue this endeavor.

It's been fun! Keep up the good birding and I hope that you enjoy this "novel" journey as much as I have enjoyed traveling it with you.

If you would like to share any of your own birding experiences and adventures, it would be my pleasure to hear from you.

Have fun!
Connie
a.k.a. "The Barbeau Birder"

TABLE OF CONTENTS

Chapter One

Common Loon

God's area code

This is all about bird watching, of course, a hobby that many of us share an interest in and participate in on different levels at different times. I have found that people come in all sorts of interesting shapes, sizes, and personalities. Their bird interests vary from the highly excitable to the calmer-than-calm bird reporter. Some folks are thrilled just to have someone to share their bird-watching experiences and sightings with and others may contact me to boast about what birds they have coming in that nobody else has. And they have every right to boast - how exciting for them!

If I have learned nothing else, it is that we all see different birds at different times and that bird-watching can be a lot like going to garage sales - you know - "one person's junk is another person's treasure."

Bird-watching is also a very chancy event - being in the right place at the right time is what birding is ALL about. I cannot tell you how many times I have arrived at an auspicious location just to be told, "Oh, that bird was just here five minutes ago!" or how many times I have said that phrase to other people as well (my bad!).

Indeed, the blink of an eye is all it takes sometimes to either see or not see a particular bird. If you look through your binoculars, you miss the broader picture, but if you put them down, then you miss the intricacies of a birds' unique coloration or unusual field marks. So how do you win in this world of bird-watching? You just have to do the best you can every day and sharing what you see with other people of like interests makes all the difference in the world. What good is seeing the rarest and most beautiful bird in the world if you are the only one who saw it?

Photographs just don't have the same effect as seeing a bird in real life. The most beautiful and spectacular of bird photographs just doesn't mean anything if someone else other than yourself saw it. While you may appreciate the beauty of the photo, you weren't there to actually observe the bird - you didn't get to enjoy the experience of that moment. Catching sight of a new bird with a friend at your side will bring you closer and give the two of you a "special moment" in time that nobody else can take away.

Come with me as I begin my journey into the limelight of our little world up here in Michigan's beautiful Eastern Upper Peninsula, what the locals call "God's country." Didn't you know that 906 is God's area code?

Learn something new

There is so much information about the bird world that I want to convey that I find myself getting impatient at times while writing this. Birds are such fascinating, interesting, constantly changing creatures that I want to absorb every little tiny detail about them. Then I want to pass on that information to my readers (who I consider my friends!), who seem to be eager to share their own information with me as well.

I have found that I certainly do NOT know everything. Isn't this one of the very basic things we learn in life? That we don't know everything - that is a lesson that is imparted to me just about every day of my life. The more I learn, the more I find out that I don't know. Therefore, learning every day is just a matter of keeping my eyes and ears open and listening to those around me that know more than I do. I once talked with a wise elderly lady who told me the secret to her long life was that she tried to learn something new every day.

What wonderful, sage advice! The day we stop trying to learn is the first day that we start to die. Indeed, the scientists tell us that the brain needs to be constantly stimulated so that it maintains its vital electrical connections. Essential neural pathways must be kept open by frequent usage. I have tried to make that one of my life's mantras - to learn something new each day. I have found that even people with personalities that I don't care for can teach me a bit of advice - even if it ends up being something that I should avoid or an action that I don't care to repeat.

How this pertains to bird-watching is that I have found that people are at all different stages of expertise when it comes to birds. Some people know very little about birds but want to learn more; some act like they know it all but actually know just enough to make themselves seem intelligent; and others, usually the most knowledgeable, do know a lot of bird information but have a tendency to keep to themselves.

Even though I write a column about birds, I profess to be only a novice. I actually have fewer birds on my life list than many of the people that read my column! The key difference may be that I make it a point to constantly learn more about birds and in the writing process I pass along anything new I have learned.

I have also found that my own views on various issues are going to be challenged. Will everyone that reads my column agree with me? Of course not. That is what makes life interesting - the fact that I want to challenge people's ideas about the world around them and if they disagree with my opinion - then that is great! There are definitely times when people do not like or may not agree with what I write, and in this great land of ours, everybody's opinion is valued and every voice can be heard. That is why not only will I be putting in excerpts from the letters of people that see eye-to-eye with me, but also some opposing voices that disagree with what I have to say. All of it is interesting and the varied viewpoints of so many different types of people is fascinating. I find that when people oppose my own viewpoints I learn a little something, maybe even something I didn't know the day before. In other words, they often open my mind to a different way of thinking that I may not have considered before.

More often than not, I find that people open my eyes to many things which I have never considered. Sometimes it's more like a slap in the face - but one which I probably needed. If we are all able to learn even the smallest bit of information about birds that we didn't know yesterday, then my goal has been achieved.

Life lists

I was recently asked a question about life lists. What are they? Who uses them and what are they for? I admit to having a hard time answering the questions because a life list is a very personal thing and it is different for everybody.

I know an elderly couple that keep a life list, but they limit their findings to what they see in their own backyard. Their "Backyard Life List" comprises over 50 years of birding in one location only. Even with this limitation, the variances are many. Do they count birds that are flying over their backyard as well as those feeding in the yard?

The starting of a life list is a personal choice and one that must be made with your own unique lifestyle in mind. Do you travel a lot? Then perhaps your list could be a worldwide list, a statewide list or just simply a local list.

However you choose to categorize your sightings, it is simply a matter of starting one day by writing down each species of bird as you see it, what time you saw it, what the date was, and what the weathers conditions were. Your list won't look like much at first, but over the years it can get quite impressive. The detail that you choose to put into it is also up to you. You can either count the birds you've seen, the birds that you can identify by ear, or both.

When I first started birding, my life list notations consisted of a quick jot in my field guide of the date and location when I saw a particular bird. Later, I progressed to a more professional printed version to keep track of all my sightings. There are many wonderful life list guides and/or notebooks available at the bookstores.

For the computer-minded person, there are some great software programs available to help you as well. Bird Brain is a Macintosh program and in the PC format there are programs such as AVISYS Birder's Diary or Birdbase.

If a keyboard and a mouse are not your forte', then a pile of 3 x 5 notecards will work just as well. You could start with a card listing each specie of bird you see, along with the date and location.

File your cards according to bird groupings such as raptors, songbirds, shorebirds, etc., or by location if you choose.

In time, your life list will shape up to be a chronicle of your life. Similar to a diary, your life list could remind you of special events or favorite places that you long to go back to. If you have a good memory, you should be able to recall how you saw each certain bird and under what circumstances. In the process, you may remember old friends that you met for the first time or past homes that you have occupied.

A good example from my own list is the first time I saw a ring-necked pheasant. I was on summer vacation at my Grandma and Grandpa Newman's house. My sister and I were accompanying Grandpa to work that day at a water well site out in the country. As we were traveling along enjoying the morning's ride, Grandpa suddenly braked hard and backed up the truck. There on the side of the road at the edge of a corn field was a gorgeous male pheasant, head held high, standing stock still.

His brilliant red head and green neck feathers were shining iridescently in the sun and his steely gray feet and legs were paused, as if he was ready to run. Then, with no warning, he flipped his long brown tail feathers and off he ran into the corn stalks.

It was a brief encounter, and the first of many, but the memory came flooding back when I read the notation, "Male, July 1971, cornfield w/Gr. Newman" in my life list. In the years since then, I have watched my father go pheasant hunting and he always used to bring back the feet as trophies (laughing while he pulled the leg tendons to scare us).

Then, as fate would have it, I moved to the Upper Peninsula, where pheasant sightings are few.

So, as you see, a life list can be simple, or very complex. Some birders even use their lists like entries into a contest. A few of the comments that I have heard are, "I'm up to 230 birds now on my life list..." and another saying, "I hope to top 100 with the next trip

I'm taking!"

It's sometimes a matter of reaching their own personal best, or perhaps a race between friends or family members to attain the highest number of bird species.

My son-in-laws regularly go on birding trips and I believe one of the goals is to see who can put the most life birds on their list. They also keep track of the variety of birds seen on that particular trip.

Diane Porter, co-inventor of Bird Brain Life List software, sums it up nicely. She says, "Adventures that the years might have erased remain alive because they are memorialized in an entry on my Life List. It's only a list of names, places and dates, but to me my Life List reads like a novel. Every entry sings the story of my life."

Bald Eagle &
Nest Sculpture

The great challenge of bird identification

One of the most difficult things to do in bird watching is the identification of the many, many different bird species. It is challenging when you are looking through your picture window at the birds in your bird feeders, but when you step out into the wilderness and try to identify birds, it suddenly becomes much harder as the birds are even less likely to stand still than they are when you are at home.

All it takes sometimes is a puff of wind or for the sun to go behind a cloud and the birds will scatter. You will get a fleeting glimpse most of the time, so you have to learn how to identify birds by using field marks. Taking notice of the key points like size, shape, beak style, coloration, activity, and unusual markings can make or break your day. The best way is to quickly jot down those key points so that you don't forget them, because, believe me - once you go to look in your field guide all of the similar-looking birds will be your bird and you won't be able to tell them apart. My own notes usually contain cryptic information like: "black eye stripe, striped belly, robin-sized, long tail, reddish-brown back, hopping in leaves." It is SO easy to forget just one crucial marking that can positively identify your bird and sometimes you only get one look (and usually not a very long one).

Even more difficult is when someone else has seen a bird and is trying to describe it to you so that you can identify it for them. Wow - this has happened to me more times than I can remember and I very rarely have found it to be easy. When I go to ask for one of the more important details, like size or length of the bird, I usually hear, "Oh, I'm not sure, I didn't notice that."

Size IS important in the bird world - as two birds that look identical, like the downy and the hairy woodpeckers, can ONLY be told apart by their size .

In the confusing world of sparrows, a tiny little mark - like a dot on a breast or their beak color or how long their tail is or how they use it - can make the world of difference when trying to identify a species that "all look alike" at a glance.

Identifying raptors can be hard also. Many times they are only seen at a distance, or from the back or from underneath while they fly over your head. When you look to buy a bird book, if you are interested in raptors, you might want to find one that identifies them from every angle. Believe it or not - a very experienced bird-watcher can identify a raptor in flight by the way that it flies and the body and wing shape alone (super!).

It can be very hard when you first start out bird-watching as all the birds look alike! Once you start paying close attention though, you will notice slight differences, especially in the way that they feed and where they feed. After that it will become easier all the time to notice their coloration, size, length, etcetera.

It won't be long and you'll be bragging about how you can even tell a crow from a raven when they fly over your head!

Exploding pipes

One of my first striking moments with a bird occurred after I moved to the Upper Peninsula. If you can, picture this: I was living in a small one and-a-half bedroom house that sat on top of a knoll with a spot of woods to the south and the rest was an old grassy field. At the bottom of the hill I was living on, to the east about 100 feet, sat a small pond that was basically just a wide spot where School Creek gathered for a rest and spread out a little bit.

I had moved to the U.P. in March and was experiencing my first spring melt. I had heard a few Canada geese (these I knew!) fly overhead honking and figured that I must have been on some type of invisible route for the birds as they always seem to be directly over the house when I heard them. A pond-to-pond route maybe?

One morning I was walking through the house when I heard the loudest, most awful racket in the world. I crouched down (don't ask me why) because it seemed like it too was coming from overhead and I didn't know what the noise was. The sound racked through my head and echoed through the house.

My first thought was, "Oh my God! The pipes in the bathroom sound like they're gonna blow up!!" I ran to the bathroom and checked it out - but the noise wasn't coming from there - it was still coming from overhead. I ran from room to room checking out the pipes and everything that I could think of, but it was not coming from inside the house - I was sure of that!

Over and over again I heard that sound, then it started to fade off into the distance. Just on a whim, I went outside and looked around. There, about a half-mile away I saw four very large, long-winged, long-necked, and long-legged birds flying off into the distance. As I stared at them, they started to call out to one another and I recognized that sound as the pipes in my house that were going to blow up.

Wow. How could four birds make a sound that was that ear-blasting and so primitive and mechanical-sounding? I was

Sandhill Crane

amazed and went immediately to find the only bird book which I had, a *Golden's Eastern North America Field Guide*. The sandhill cranes were easy to identify and even reading about what sound they make, I would not have been prepared for them.

Even today - 18 years later - I am still frequently flabbergasted at the wonders of the birding world and the people that love the birds.

What a difference a word makes

As a non-hunter (my husband Pat would call me a tree-hugger at this point), often my view of hunting tends to be a bit jaded. While I support hunters, I don't have any plans to participate and I certainly know that I hate it when people kill animals just for the thrill of killing. I am of the old school belief that if you take an animal's life, that you should eat the meat and use any part of it that you can to avoid waste. While I try to avoid any sort of politics in my bird writings, sometimes it still sneaks into the conversation.

One week, when I failed to make the distinction between hunters and poachers, I was chastised quite roundly by one Tom P. from Sault Ste. Marie. He emphasized the difference between the two that I had never considered and opened my eyes to a viewpoint which I had never considered. Here is his letter:

"I disagree with your assertion that hunting is a contributing factor to eagle mortality. Poaching - yes, but not hunting. Hunters cease to be called hunters when they willfully shoot an eagle or anything else they shouldn't be shooting. They're poachers, the same way a motorist becomes

a criminal when he decides to drive under the influence of alcohol or drugs.

This may seem to be a minor point, but as a longtime hunter and bird enthusiast, I take exception to being lumped together with the poachers.

I am a rabid waterfowl hunter, and some think it strange that someone who shoots ducks can actually appreciate their beauty and grace in the air. But I've long contended that a duck hunter is nothing more than a birder with a gun. More often than not, we spend the day watching birds (including an eagle or two if we're hunting in the south end of Lake George or over in Little Lake George) without firing a shot. On one particularly great day, my partner and I were enjoying a huge lunch, and watching a few ducks and THREE bald eagles in the area. He declared that our hunting trip was more like a "picnic with guns."

I've always had a great appreciation for birds. Some of that appreciation was instilled in me by one of your predecessors who worked at the newspaper for years. Paul used to help me put together my weekly outdoor page when I was a reporter and he often had a 'bird report' for me. I'll never forget the day back in 1986 when he told me about a bird he'd spotted down by the Sugar Island ferry dock. It was a bird I'd never seen before, and I wasted no time in getting over to the landing to see if I could spot it from the mainland. I never did see it, but these days I can see one of those same 'rare' birds without leaving my porch. The oddity that he saw? It was a double-crested cormorant, not exactly the most rare of creatures flying up and down the St. Mary's River these days!"

Observations

Over the years, I have heard and read many, many bird reports. Most are simple and consist of what people are seeing coming in to their bird feeders or their back yards.

Every now and then, I get an odd report with birds or conditions that are baffling to me as well. All of the reports are interesting, some fascinating and others downright bizarre.

It seems as if the natural world is much more complex than I ever thought it would be and there are things that go on when we are not looking that would amaze every one of us.

Missing Feathers

• One January day I received a letter from Daryl F. He had a small flock of ruffed grouse that were coming in to feed in the flowering crabapple trees in his yard. He wrote: *"One of the three grouse that have been visiting appears to have lost all of its long tail feathers and its rump is covered with just the short feathery ones. I was wondering if it could have lost them by being frozen in while nesting in a snowbank overnight (I don't think so) or could a fox or other animal have experienced a mouthful of feathers while the grouse had a near death experience (I think this more likely). This bird seems to have more difficulty balancing while moving from branch to branch than the other two."*

Eagle Wonder

• Another reader named Bill B. emailed me regularly with reports about our National Symbol: the Bald Eagle. He was lucky enough to be renting a house high up on the clay banks alongside the St. Marys River and had great eagle viewing. One day he wrote: *"I lived on Kodiak Island for 3 years and we had the pleasure of seeing them many times. I remember one time we tried to count the number sitting in a tree and quit at 50 because we couldn't make an accurate count. It was so beautiful when they would fly down to the river and pick up a salmon and fly off with it. First of all it seemed like they would drop 10 to 15 feet as they became airborne from their weight and had to get some airspeed up before they could fly. After diving into the water they*

Bald Eagle

would pick up a salmon and knew almost immed
with it. If it was too big they just dropped it and
got another one. All of this took maybe 30 second
never forget.

Now I have an opportunity to watch them aga
banks in August and had 2 pair that flew by my h
At least I saw them almost every day I was home. I was telling my neighbor about them and don't really think he believed me. One day sitting at my table visiting he just about broke my arm. He spotted 2 males about 30 feet away, just hovering, watching the water. He now is a believer. Amazing how they move their head to see the water. I never knew why until I read your article today. How interesting. I believe they are 2 pair because I have also seen the females quite a few times, one at a time. Along with that thought, I have found 2 nests with my telescope. They are now gone for the winter as I have been watching the nests every chance I get and have spotted ravens sitting on the edge of one of them. The eagles always return to their original nests, right? Something as beautiful as they are has to be shared."

Swan Landing

• This report came through e-mail from Dave S. and I found it very interesting: *"We live at the Neebish Island Ferry landing and see a variety of birds. February 3rd and 4th a pair of mute swans were on the ice near open water. On the 11th a robin on a post next to the river. The 12th a falcon - probably a merlin - near 14 mi. & Riverside Drive. Have*

Mute Swan

es around lately, earlier than usual. Promise of spring?
anks for the article you published on the ravens. I read somewhere
t they have been known to live up to 80 years. When I lived in
Munising I mentioned this to the operator of the landfill and he quickly
pointed out a raven and said, 'There's one right there. He doesn't have a
feather on his head,' and sure enough, he was bald. Keep your eyes open.
Birds have to be one of our greatest treasures."

Bullies

We humans tend to think that it is only the human race that has bullies in its world, but that is not entirely true. The bird world has bullies also, but usually for good reason...

Crow Harassment

• This email from Al D. got me thinking about birds and bird bullies: *"Had an interesting observation yesterday. Was going to a friends house and I spotted two crows harassing a hawk on the ground that I at first glance thought was an owl. I turned around and went back to check and it was two crows harassing a Harrier (Marsh Hawk) that had a partially eaten snowshoe hare. They were really working it over but at a safe distance but within two feet. I stepped out of my van to take a picture with my tele but they all three flew away. The Harrier with its rabbit and the crows right with it. I noticed another hawk, probably the mate sitting up in a tree making no attempt to help out. I have never witnessed this behavior before."*

Al was right - there was some harassment going on, but it was simply a matter of survival. The crows wanted to get a meal out of the harrier's meal but knew that they would be a meal if they weren't careful!

Crows have been harassing owls, hawks, and eagles since they've been alive. I found it odd once that the crows and ravens were so persistent about it until I found out why.

Crows will dive-bomb an owl that is sleeping in the daytime on its roost and they will do close fly-bys of eagles and hawks to annoy them. And they do it over and over again! It seems that the crows are trying to get a potential predator out of their "territory" and move it on into another bird's territory. Great horned owls are one of the largest predators of young crows in the nest so it would make sense that the adults would try to drive them away if they can.

Sometimes bird watchers will listen for a flock of crows that sound like they are harassing something - this is a possible location of a bird of prey and the birders will drive to that spot to check it out. More often than not there is a raptor nearby if it can be spotted - often it will be taking cover inside deep brush or a thick tree.

Why I write

I don't write a birding column for the recognition. Nor do I write it for the money (there is none). Instead I do it strictly for personal satisfaction. I learn about the birds the same way that everyone else does - through trial and error. I find things out through observation, searching, and research. If I don't know what that bird is, then I find out.

The reason that I keep writing about birds is that people seem to identify with what I write. I hope that they believe that I am just an average person who shares their love of birds and that they will use me for a sounding board to report what they are seeing and to answer questions. I won't go so far as to use the "expert" word, because I am far from it. For, you see, I too have foibles. I too make mistakes. Have I ever misidentified a bird? Definitely! Will I do it again? Probably. I am human!

That is the nature of this birding business - the flexibility and the uncertainty. If I tell you something specific about birds, then the birds have to prove me wrong. And they often do. If I state that the field guides say a certain bird won't show up in our area, then the bird will be there thumbing his nose at me when I go to identify it.

Along the way, I find myself having FUN! I have met what feels like hundreds of interesting people from all over the world in this hobby. Many of them have been at our house, watched the birds in my own backyard and been thrilled to do so. I enjoy my correspondence with every single person and am happy to report that "sharing" is alive and well in the bird-watching community. I think that I have come into contact with just about every personality type there is and it is interesting to see what drives people and what their interests are.

Here is a letter from Jarl H. : *"Very quickly (before the mailman comes) I wish to comment on your new series in the local newspaper regarding local birds. Great!*

Pileated Woodpecker

I am a senior (senile) citizen who is retired at my old homestead on Sugar Island. I am not one of the respected 'birders,' but I was introduced to the 'disease' by a legitimate birder before I retired. Hence, my curiousity persists.

So, after having read one of your articles in the News, *I'm sending the enclosed photo, which you may keep. It was taken through the kitchen window, hence the fuzziness."*

Mystery birds

One of the toughest things that a person can do is to try to identify something that someone else has seen. And I've got to believe that birds are even tougher than the usual subjects. Every time that it happens I give it the old college try and make an attempt at identifying the bird - but it is really hard!

It's not like I can see the bird myself. Usually when I hear the description, there is a key factor missing. Although people do their very best at remembering the bird's details, you tend to remember what is important to you. For instance, they may tell me what color the bird is and where its markings are, but they can't tell me if it is robin-sized or chickadee-sized!

There are some people though, that are very good at relaying bird information and these are a delight to help them with identification. I wish there were a simpler way of doing it - like having a chart that everyone knew to use or a check-off list, but that's just wishful thinking.

There are basics to bird identification but the trouble is remem-

Juvenile
Cooper's Hawk

bering them. Oftentimes excitement over seeing the bird is a factor. Then there is the fact that usually when we see a mystery bird we have about three or four seconds - that doesn't help.

The basics involve only a few items: overall size, body shape, color, identifying marks, and behavior. If you have time, observe the bird for as long as you can and jot down some quickie notes. Things like: size is like an X, shape is like an X, mask across eyes, black wings with yellow bars, white rump, feeds on ground, likes thistle seed, tiny bill, large unfeathered feet, etc.

For example, a gray jay looks a lot like a shrike. They have the same body size and coloration. BUT! The shrike has a black mask on its face and a hooked bill. The jay is reclusive and shy and the shrike is bold and usually sits at the tippy top of a tree to hunt from. The gray jay also is colored almost exactly like a black-capped chickadee. The only difference is the size!

Bird identification is tough enough when you get a nice long look at the bird or are able to take a picture of it. However, doing it over the phone or through the mail is just about impossible - though I continue to try!

Here's an example:

Janice K. wrote: *"Now here is a question - how good are you at identifying 'mystery birds?' This is the situation:*

About 1:30 pm, Jerry and I were driving north on Lower Hay Lake Road between 7 and 8 Mile. I got all excited because I thought I saw an eagle in a very tall tree at the edge of a field by the bridge on Sailor's Creek (runs to the St. Marys). The bird sat up like an eagle or hawk and was quite tall. As we watched, it flew to the west. While sitting, the bird had a white head and dark body. In flight, the bird was all white - the only identification marking was a large black spot in the center of each white wing (seen from underneath). I have just about worn the poor bird book out looking for something close! In flight it had a large wing span, but not enough for an eagle - maybe 3 1/2 to 4 1/2 feet. The wing beats were long and slow - not 'flappy.' I checked the osprey which my head says it must be, but the black area was not at the edge of the wing 'wrist' or bend as the flight picture shows. Also, the osprey has a lot of black feathers that we did not see. There have been ospreys seen in the area in the summer.

You are going to think I am nuts, but the picture that is the closest to what we saw is a kite! I know, I know, that isn't possible. Okay, I accept that, but do you have ANY idea as to what we were seeing? Our friends in the area said they had been watching a short-eared owl the same day, and they tried to convince me that it was the same bird. The one we saw had no color underneath except for the black wing spots centered on white wings, and the head was definitely white or very light.

This will bug me until I see it again or identify it - one or the other. Any help you can offer would be appreciated."

This particular time the identification wasn't too bad, as I had had this question come up before. The bird in question was a light phase rough-legged hawk, which looks like a miniature bald eagle from afar. The rough-legged is a very large buteo with a giant wingspan for a hawk, so it is commonly mistaken for an eagle when viewed from a distance, or from the air. The giveaway is the black "wrist patches" which, along with a white rump, are one of the trademark identification tips for a rough-legged.

Chapter Two

Wearing a watch

One winter, I think it was in the late 1990s, our house became "sort-of" famous.

Great gray owls were a rarity in Michigan, but every six or seven years they would come down from Canada in the irruption years. These were the years where prey was scarce during the winter and the lemming population had plummeted. These conditions meant that the northern owls came down to the United States in great numbers looking for food. Great gray owls, snowy owls, and sometimes, saw-whets would appear out of nowhere in Upper Michigan, Wisconsin, and Minnesota. For those who live downstate (lower Michigan) and in other more southernly states, this was a treat to get to see an Arctic owl.

It just so happened that during one of these irruption years we were out looking and saw large numbers of great gray owls (which are always impressive to see) in the area. We saw them on Neebish Island, Sugar Island, and in many spots around the Eastern Upper Peninsula.

One of the spots where we began to see them regularly was our own front yard. We were thrilled, of course, and took to watching them come in every day to hunt the mice and voles that would be tunneling around in the snow underneath our bird feeders.

Now, you'd have to see one of these owls to understand our fascination with them. Not only are they indescribably beautiful with their color mottling and patterning, but they allowed you to look at them without flying away - unlike most raptors.

Before we knew it, word had spread that we had great gray owls on our property and many of our bird-watching friends came over to see and photograph them. The beauty of this whole event is that the grays have no fear of humans. This allowed even those with simple and inexpensive cameras to be able to stand practically directly underneath the owl and still get a great photograph. The great gray owls were definitely "camera friendly." They would allow you to approach, but didn't put up with a lot of noise - they were hunting after all and were trying to listen for their dinner.

The grays were at our place on an irregular basis, but one large adult made daily visits to our front yard, where he would arrive almost exactly every evening about five-o'clock. It made no sense to look for him earlier, as he was never there.

By this time we had gotten word that someone had put our address on a birding website as "a definite place to find a great gray owl." It wasn't long before we had cars and trucks pulling into our driveway every day looking for their own glance at a gorgeous owl. We were amenable and agreed to let many come in to our home and warm up for a bit after they had stood outside in the freezing cold taking photographs. It was a time of great fun and we met people from all over the United States who had made special plans to come up and see the irruption for themselves.

Great Gray Owl

One car that we particularly remembered was a group of four little old ladies. It was about one o'clock in the afternoon on a clear, cold winter day when they whipped their little rental car into our driveway. Husband Pat was working in his workshop near the end of the driveway when he heard them pull up. He went out to greet them. As he began to talk with them (they had all the windows down so they could all listen and talk at once), he found out that they were avid bird-watchers and that they had found our address online. They had flown up here all the way from Virginia and had rented a car at the airport to drive around and look for winter birds.

One of the ladies asked, "Where's the great gray owl?" Pat replied, "Well, he usually doesn't fly in until just before dark, usually about five o'clock."

A voice spoke up from the back seat, "Yeah right, like he wears a watch!" Then they all rolled up their windows, put the car into drive and backed out of the driveway. No thank-you, no good-bye, no piss-on-you, no nothing.

Pat stood there flabbergasted for a minute or two, then shook his head and walked back into the workshop. It was a strange interchange, but he had told them what they needed to know.

That very evening, at exactly five minutes before five o'clock, a large, beautiful great gray owl silently flew into the yard and landed on top of the bird feeder. He proceeded to look around from his perch and to search for his nightly Ridge Road dinner.

He was undisturbed in his hunting, as nobody came back to look for him that night.

Sharing the sightings through photographs

It's just about impossible to be everywhere at once, isn't it? One of the neatest things about writing a birding column is that I get to "see" what others are seeing. People send me photographs and email me digital pictures and these photos sometimes come in rare and unusual forms.

I enjoy every single photo that is sent to me, and it is a neat way for me to share your sightings with you. I may not be sitting in your kitchen sipping a cup of coffee while we look through the windows together, but I can sure imagine you doing that and in that sense I am there with you. Some photos are serious and capture a brief moment in time that will never be seen again. Other photos are of common birds in uncommon places - like on your head or hand. And even more photos are just plain bizarre. I can never say "thank you" enough to everyone that sends me photographs - as they are all a delight. Here are just a few samples of some neat photos that have been sent to me...

Snowy Breakfast
• From Howard A. in Pickford: *"I am sending you this snapshot I took of the sharptails that come to our home every morning for their breakfast. They come to our back door and I throw them out their food. I*

really enjoy your column and thought you'd enjoy the picture."

Sharp-tail Grouse

• From Jarl H. of Sugar Island: *"A red-breasted nuthatch in hand is better than two on the feeder."* and *"A Sugar Island yellow-birch owl at its lodge."*

Red-breasted Nuthatch

Yellow Birch

Bird identification

Another bird to help identify...

* From Dolores G. in Sault Ste. Marie: *"I saw what I thought was an unusual bird for this area. Its color was about the color of this smiley face sticker (sticker was enclosed). It was yellow all-over except the wings I think. Its tail was rather long. Its wings were either gray or beige. Its body was rather thin looking. It had a light yellow beak and a rather longish, thin neck - small bird. It seemed longer from the tip of the beak to the end of its tail than a canary, by far. There were other canary-type birds around. This was not one. The sighting was at about 4:30 PM. It was raining, without any sunshine so the color on the wings were hard to distinguish exactly. Do you have any idea what this bird might be?"*

Shy birds

There is something about raptors - they are shy. I have decided that they definitely do NOT like to have their picture taken. You can drive by a hawk high up on top of a utility pole many times, but as soon as you slow down, then it will take off and fly away. We have had this happen to us so many times that it isn't funny.

I have also heard from many, many people who have had the same problem. You wouldn't be able to think that a hawk or an owl would pay attention to how fast you are driving, but I tell you that if you go by at 50 mph and then turn around and go by at 30 mph that bird will fly away every time before you can get there. They usually fly just as I'm getting my camera out the window and starting to bring the bird into focus. You can imagine how many pictures I have of bird rumps flying away from me!

So how does one go about solving this issue? The professionals will tell you that you have to stalk the bird. In other words, they will follow the raptor each time that it flies away and keep following it every time until it gets tired and used to them, then they can take its picture. I don't know about you, but that sounds exhausting.

It also sounds like it could be difficult, as usually the bird will fly onto someone's property, and you have to ask permission to go onto their property to pursue the bird. Either that or you end up in a mucky swamp with no boots, get sucked into some unexpected quicksand, or get so twisted around that you don't know in which direction your car is located. That doesn't sound like very much fun to me.

I'll just keep trying to be faster than they are and get my camera out faster. Maybe in time I will find that magical mile-per-hour that I can drive by where they won't fly and where I can still squeeze off a camera shot. Maybe.

Merrie N. from Sault Ste. Marie phrased the situation quite well: *"I must tell you that those hawks are so elusive. I swear they can read your mind that you are even thinking of taking their picture. As soon as you reach for the camera, they fly away from their perches."*

Sharing observations

Peeping Crane
• From Phil Y. of Sault Ste. Marie: *"We were in Florida two weeks ago visiting some friends who live on a golf course. One afternoon we looked out the back door and there was a sandhill crane looking in. We put out a pile of birdseed and he walked up to about 2 feet from us waiting for us to back off from the bird seed. That night he walked off across the golf course and started calling (a most unusual sound). He was waiting for breakfast the next day and hung around until afternoon. He was gone the next."*

Geese vs. Autos
• From Daryl F. in Sault Ste. Marie: *"Since I play a lot of golf I am sorry to see so many pairs of geese on the course when I go on my morning walk. It seems as if there are more and more every year and have become a local nuisance. It bothers me to see the people feeding them at the boat launch across from the course because of all the droppings that are going to be left around. This encourages them and helps to make them tame. I am surprised that there have been any automobile accidents with them strolling across the road and people having to stop for them along*

those curves."

A Pair Sharing

• From Bill B. in Sault Ste. Marie: *"A Male Eagle spends time sitting on top of its nest so proudly. Just beautiful. He is sitting there right now but will be gone in a minute or so as he doesn't stay there long. I'm assuming the female is now sitting on her eggs as he makes a lot of trips there and sometimes I can see his head bobbing down into the nest. Is he feeding her? I wonder. Yesterday I couldn't find him anyplace by the nest almost all day and about 4 yesterday afternoon I moved the telescope just a hair by mistake while looking in it and it stopped on the Eagle sitting on top of a dead White Birch a ways away. Hard to judge distance when it's through the telescope. He was sitting facing into the wind and I could see his tail feathers moving to help him keep his balance. How lucky can I be."*

Incredible black bird

I was walking down a snow-covered trail recently behind our house when I saw something black up on the trail ahead. "What is that?" I wondered. "A piece of bark? A garbage bag? What could it be?" As I got closer wonder soon turned to amazement. It was a raven laying dead on the trail, and a very large raven at that.

I bent over to examine it and thought about all the times that I had seen ravens in the past. Ravens were common in the Upper Peninsula, but not so much in the winter. Most of them usually migrated a bit south, but we had been having such a mild winter that I'm sure that they had decided to stick around - especially if they were still finding food here and there.

Ravens are easy to spot, with their large body, heavy beak and jet-black feathers. Sometimes it can be difficult to determine whether it is a raven or a crow you are seeing, but then they fly and the raven's spade-shaped tail is distinctive in flight.

I had seen quite a few ravens and have always been fascinated by the variety of their calls. They can make more noises than you can imagine and a few of them are quite surprising as they have a large voice tonal range.

This was historic. It was the first time I had seen a raven up close and personal. I couldn't believe the size! If this particular raven had not been dead, then I think I would have been a bit afraid of it due to its size. It was simply the biggest black bird I had ever seen.

Common Raven

Its feet were quite long and the talons on its toes were enough to make any raptor jealous. The talons were easily a half-inch long and could have punctured through my hand if it had been alive.

A close examination of the raven's corpse brought no clues as to how it had died. It almost looked like it had just fallen out of the sky. Its eyes (if they had still been there) were wide open and there was a small amount of snow on its breast - like it had just died mid-air and took a dive to the ground. It was stiff (it was winter after all) and no predators had showed an interest in it so far.

My goodness - you should have seen its beak. It was massive and easily three to four inches long. All in all, I was very impressed by its size. I knew that ravens were big - but good grief - this was a giant!

Out of all the places that a raven could have chosen to die, this was an opportune place for me to be able to check one out. I picked it up - it didn't weigh that much but its wings were large from what I could tell. It was in rigor of course and I was only able to open its wings a small amount - but it was easy to project that this bird easily had at least a three-foot wingspan.

You might think that this is all so very gruesome. How could I touch a dead raven? Well, how could I not? It was a great opportunity and I also had some latex gloves in my pocket so all was cool. I touched its beak in amazement and even tried to open it (no luck). I put my fingers inside of its talons to see how much damage it could do to me if it were alive.

The most amazing thing about this raven was its cleanliness. I have always thought in my mind that carrion eaters would be filled with dirt and grime and other disgusting things. I found just the opposite. This bird was a beautiful shiny black, almost iridescent in its blackness. Its entire body was spectacularly clean and well groomed. There was not a speck of dirt on the entire bird, nor did it smell bad or seem gross in any way.

All in all, I considered myself lucky to be able to examine such a treasure so closely. A raven is a meticulously clean, well-groomed bird and its size is truly amazing.

Identifying a bird by its call

I once attended a birding seminar down at the DNR's Conference Center in Roscommon. It was a wonderful time and we saw many great birds on our trips into the woods and the surrounding grasslands. A great time was spent rubber-necking all day and we were glad to sit down for dinner that night. It's hard to describe how much fun it is to bird-watch with a large group of people. There are always different hushed conversations happening at the same time and a person can learn so much just from listening to other people.

Later that evening I was sitting in the middle of about 25 people and we were all listening to a speech about bird vocalizations. The material was fascinating and I was wondering how I was going to be able to remember it all. The speaker was using phonics of a sort as a teaching tool. Basically he was breaking down the bird calls into easily-rememberable English words. Some of them are quite easy and we already know them - the "chick-a-dee-dee-dee" of a chickadee or the "jay! jay!" call of an alarmed bluejay.

Many other calls were more complex but he had a delightful way of breaking down the sounds. One of the calls could be the common yellowthroat with its "witchety, witchety, witchety" call while it is hidden in a thick bush or the "po-ta-to-chip, po-ta-to-chip" call of the goldfinch in flight.

I learned a lot that day and wish I could remember more of his call breakdowns. I suppose I could make up my own if I really wanted to.

After the speech, the speaker took questions for a while. A man with two hearing aids stood up and pleaded with the speaker: "I hope you can help me. Ever since I got my hearing aids I have found that my birds have gotten all messed up. I find that I can hear a mosquito fart but I can't hear a grasshopper sparrow! What can I do?" How do you answer that one?

Listers

There are always different types of bird watchers out there. They all have different criteria for adding birds to their life lists. For some I wonder if it isn't the challenge itself, rather than the bird that is their goal. Are they so wrapped up in the competition that they don't really care about the bird? I'm sure there are a few people like this. These would be the people that come to see a rare bird, and as soon as they've sighted it in their binoculars, they tell their companion, "OK, I've got it. Let's go now." And I've met quite a few of these type of people in the last decade or so.

For me, and for many others I am sure, bird-watching is all about the birds themselves. What they do, how they act, what their habitat is, who they hang around with, what they eat, etcetera. Observation is simply that - observing the bird and remembering its characteristics so that hopefully you'll be able to identify it the next time you see it.

Some people are good at remembering what a bird sounds like or identifying it from its body shape. I am a bit more stubborn. I require good long looks, and lots of them, to lock the bird's identity into my brain. I try to memorize what it does, where it is feeding, and what other types of birds it is hanging out among.

It may seem as if it is all just a big game, and maybe it is, but most of us treat it light-heartedly and catch what glimpses we can.

Some bird-watchers are oh-so-serious about this giant competition that we are all in. And what do they get in the end? Is someone going to give them a medal if they see so many birds? No. Are they going to get national or statewide recognition if they see a lot of birds? No. It's a competition, yes, but it is with ourselves. It is a "personal best" competition - something to strive for and a personal goal to reach if we can.

Nobody will give us a medal when we hit the 200, 300, or 400 mark on our life lists, but maybe we'll get a clap on the back from a fellow bird-watcher or a handshake of congratulations. The birding life list is something incongruous. It's nothing we can prove nor does it fit into a neat category of filing. For instance, we don't have drawers full of the birds that we've seen, nor photographs of every single bird every single time that we've seen them.

All we have are our memories and our checklists. Most of us have simple life lists that we check off. Others are a bit more fanatical and have life lists, day lists, backyard lists, vacation lists, travel lists, wish lists and, just maybe, armchair lists. It's all about having fun and enriching our lives with one of the things that gives us joy and is totally free - watching birds.

Favorite birds

Why is it that we determine some birds to be our favorites and not others? It would seem that if you loved birds, that you would love all birds. I have, however, found that not to be true. We all have our favorites, but some more than others. What most of us have discovered is that birds have personalities too. Some are gentle and non-obtrusive, while others are bullies and scare off all of the other birds at the bird feeders. Some birds are gregarious and others are loners. In our heart of hearts we are always rooting for the "little guy" and we tend to dislike the bullies.

Take blue jays for instance. Aren't they a gorgeous blue bird? They are a wonder of color in bright blue, soft lavender, and slashes of black and white mixed in with the other colors. We love to look at them, but their behavior is obnoxious. The blue jays routinely push the other birds off of the bird feeders and they flare their wings when they fly in so that the smaller birds scatter. Not only that, but they like to make a habit of boldly flying through the trees hollering and also doing fly-bys on the bird feeders so that the others think that it is a hawk flying through.

And then - to make matters worse - they are simply pigs. When we feed the birds, we would like to think that it will last a few days. With the blue jays around, it will not last long. We have watched a single blue jay stuff over 50 black-oil sunflower seeds into its throat pouch and then be so laden down that it could hardly fly away. That is year round too! I would feel better if I knew that they were feeding young chicks, but the fact remains that we truly don't know where they take the seeds or what they do with them. All we do know for a fact is that they are back to get more seed in less than a minute. That is a good description of pigginess!

Blue Jay

Specialties

There are literally hundreds of different species of birds and each has its own method of survival. Some birds eat seeds, some eat worms, some eat insects, some eat meat, and others eat carrion. Birds' interests have diverged into hundreds of different "specialties" which they use to survive.

Over the years I have seen many different kinds of food being eaten; some of which surprise me yet today. I also am aware that there are birds all over the world that I will never see that have even more exotic tastes.

In our own backyard, I sometimes see chickadees or other small birds flitting through the bare bushes on a sunny day in the wintertime. There may be snow all around them everywhere, but they appear to be buzzing through the branches picking off unknown things. What could they be eating? Tiny snow fleas? Little bits of leaves? Whatever it is, it is something that my giant eyes cannot see. I will have to investigate this matter in more detail. When I go outside to see what it is - there is nothing there! Maybe they have eaten it all...

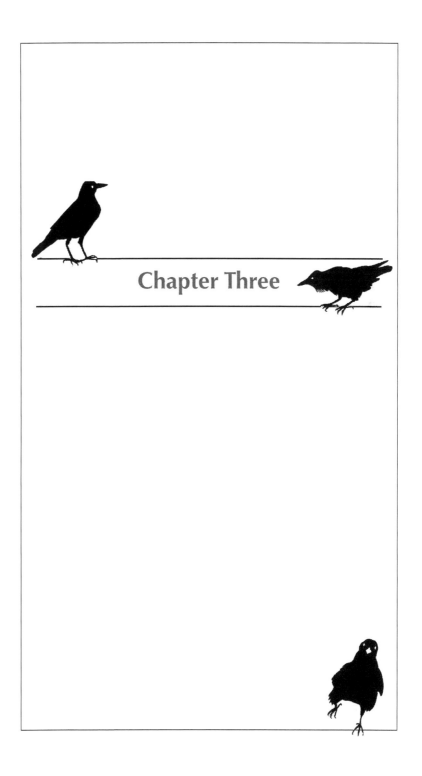

Chapter Three

Twitchers

At one time, bird-watchers were known as "bird geeks." Our hobby was frowned upon, especially because we had a tendency to point binoculars at people's houses (which made them understandably nervous - even though it was their bird feeders we were focused on) and drive real slow past your house if you even had one bird feeder out in your front yard. Little did people know then how harmless we really were.

Now this was probably 30 or so years ago that this mentality prevailed. Nowadays people seem to be much more informed about bird-watchers, though there are still a few backward folks that zip out onto their front porch with a shotgun if they see someone they don't know pull into their driveway unannounced.

Today bird-feeding and bird-watching are even higher in popularity than all of the types of hunting combined. Many more people feed birds and watch them than will head into the woods to shoot them during various times of the year. Most interestingly enough, quite often the two hobbies combine. You may have someone who feeds the birds, but shoots the ones that he or she doesn't like - the so-called nuisance birds. OR you may have someone who feeds the birds in their backyard but also enjoys going small-game hunting to take pheasants, grouse, or snipe (yes, that's a real bird) for their own consumption.

In Europe, bird-watchers are sometimes called "twitchers," and are often mistaken for spies, according to the *London Daily Telegraph*. Rumor has it that this nickname came about because the bird-watchers became so excited when they saw a rare bird that they started to tremble - or to twitch - in their anticipation to see more of the bird. It is said that those who travel long distances to see a rare bird do so to TICK (check off) that bird from a list. Other names for rare bird-watchers included pot-hunters, tally-hunters, and tick-hunters. Luckily, in the United States today nobody thinks about spies coming to their house and a bird-watcher has become more of a novelty than a rarity.

Wikipedia today tells us that "the main goal of twitching is often to accumulate species on one's lists. Some birders engage in competition to accumulate the longest species list. The act of the pursuit itself is referred to as a twitch or a chase. A rare bird that stays put long enough for people to see it is twitchable or chaseable." If you aren't confused enough, check this out: "If a twitcher fails to see a rare bird, they have dipped out; if other twitchers do see the bird, he may feel gripped off. Suppression is the act of concealing news of a rare bird from other twitchers."

Bird-watching is one of the fastest growing hobbies in North America and is second only to gardening. It has been documented that there are more than 63 million people (in just the United States!) who watch birds and bird-watching is the fastest growing outdoor activity in America. Some people bird-watch on the sly, secretly locating birds, but telling no one. Other people are blatant about it and travel all around the country hoping to catch a glimpse of one particular bird or another. Some even travel the world, going to exotic corners, trying to get as many birds on their life list as possible.

Studies have shown that the numbers are equally divided between men and women when it comes to bird-watchers. And also that the average age of bird-watchers is all across the board. I have known very intense bird watchers who were only nine or ten years old and have also met fanatical bird-watchers who were in their 80s and still pursuing their love of birds.

When does it happen?

When does one officially become a bird-watcher? I don't believe that there is any specific time or place, but that it is a gradual effect. It's usually not a one-day-you-don't-notice-birds and then the next day you do. Bird-watching is a sneaky hobby - you gradually become a bird-watcher, usually without your conscious knowledge.

Sometimes it feels sudden, as you notice a bright bird near your vehicle or out your window at work. Maybe a friend shows you what exciting birds they have coming in to their bird feeder or maybe you notice somebody watching birds and are intrigued to find out just what they find so interesting.

I remember as a small child my Grandpa Newman would have a sort of "station" beside one of the windows in his living room. There next to his favorite armchair was a TV tray. On that tray was a small, worn pair of binoculars and a bird field guide. From his comfy seat he had an ideal spot to keep an eye on his lone bird feeder. Even though this feeder was in "the middle of nowhere" so to speak, it still attracted its portion of birds. There were no bushes for cover, nor was there a birdbath anywhere close that I remember. Instead, there were empty fields surrounding the house and a neat, closely cropped lawn that held the bird feeder near the house. While my childhood was an awfully long time ago, I can still remember Grandpa pointing out the yellow and red birds to me. My retention was less than ideal, but I am sure that he was trying to show me the wonders of the bird world and what a delight they were to him. Could it have been then that my love of birds began?

Bird Statues

During my many years of watching birds I have observed quite a few interesting behaviors. Sometimes I can explain them, and other times I can't. We're all learning all the time, right?

One behavior that continues to intrigue me is when birds turn into statues. What is that?, you might ask. Well, sometimes you're watching the birds at the bird feeders when you notice that almost all the birds flush out all of a sudden. A few birds are left - probably the ones with slow reflexes - and something weird happens to them. They freeze in position and they do not move a single feather.

One example of this was what happened on a fine winter day at our backyard bird feeders. I was watching a cute little pine siskin while it was sitting huddled at our thistle feeder. I began to think that maybe it was sick, as it hadn't moved for four or five minutes. Before I went outside to check on it, I started looking around in the trees. Aha! There in a nearby pine tree was a northern shrike. As I watched, the shrike blasted off of its branch to pursue a black-capped chickadee.

The shrike spent the next three minutes hovering around the large pine tree, changing positions every few seconds, while the chickadee zipped from branch to branch way inside where the larger shrike couldn't get to.

Eventually the shrike gave up the chase and then the chickadee flew out and joined the 'statue' of a siskin. Both then began to feed normally, like nothing had ever happened.

Most predators do not have a developed sense of smell and they hunt by eyesight alone. So if you aren't moving, it makes sense that a raptor would not be able to see you!

A tree near the bird feeder, would have given the siskin more of a chance, but as it was, his statue game was more than enough defense.

What is it about bald eagles?

Maybe it is just the fact that they are our national symbol, I don't know. The bald eagle has achieved a certain status in our mind. It is without doubt a majestic and graceful bird. When viewed up close, it is an incredibly large bird.

I thank our lucky stars that Benjamin Franklin was not successful in his bid to have the turkey voted as our national bird. That just would not have cut it in my mind - the turkey is not majestic, nor is it graceful. If you have ever watched a turkey run, you have to laugh. They are splay-legged and run with all sorts of things flapping around and with their feathers shifting from side to side on their body.

The eagle on the other hand fixes you in its gaze and you find yourself being weighed and measured. Its heavily-browed golden eyes stare intently at you and seem to probe into your entire being. Its eyes are so large in proportion to its skull that it does not have the room for muscles to move the eyeballs. Instead, the eagle must move its entire head to look around.

The bald eagle is one of those birds that does NOT have to blend into its environment in order to survive. It has few natural enemies and it can sport a shining white head and tail as a sign of its magnificence.

We have been within 20 to 50-feet of a bald eagle many times and I have been amazed at them every time. They hold a sense of power within their body and once you catch sight of their long talons, you can easily imagine how they are able to snatch a slippery, squirmy fish.

Even non-bird lovers are amazed to see an eagle. It doesn't matter if they are feeding on a carcass on the side of the road or sitting high up in a tree alongside the highway, there is a magnetism there that makes you slow down your car for a closer look. Just remember that an eagle on the side of the road is often fearless of vehicles and it will not fly immediately unless it feels threatened.

As for myself, I never tire of the regal bald eagle, with all its arrogance and beauty. To see one depart from an old snag is

Bald Eagles

impressive. Its thick, heavy yellow legs, the wide soaring, almost eight-foot-wingspan and the snow-white head all combine to create an image of power and a sense of awe.

Longevity

It is never more apparent than when we have a death in the family that we are aware of our mortality. Humans do live an absurdly long time, and while I am not complaining, it is interesting how short a life birds have.

There are so many factors that come into play in how long a bird lives that it is almost too hard to figure out. Research supports the fact that the larger the bird, the longer the lifespan. In each of our lives there is a constant circle of birth, life, death, and back to birth again. Nowhere is that cycle more clear than in the world of birds. Most of the songbirds we know and love have ridiculously short lives. Chickadees and other small birds may only live three years in the wild. Birds have an incredible number of things against them like predators, disease, and weather.

When people write to me and ask, "Why aren't my usual birds here?" It's hard to describe for them all of the factors that keep birds alive. A more appropriate quote would be, "I'm amazed my birds are still alive today!"

The same songbirds that you saw a decade ago are probably four or five generations ahead of the birds that you are seeing today. Some birds, such as bluebirds and some of the early nesting songbirds, must instinctively know that their longevity is short. They make up for this by sometimes raising two or more broods per season. In like respect, larger birds like ospreys and eagles, who live longer, can afford to take a few years to mature before reproducing.

Availability of food is also a factor. Wild birds spend most of their waking hours searching for food and can consume up to 20 percent of their body weight overnight just trying to stay warm. Perhaps not only do you feed birds, but your neighbors also may so do this year for the first time. This would tend to spread out the birds in your area and make their numbers appear to be fewer.

If we could only tell them apart by their looks, we would know for sure. The opposite could also be true. If your bird-feeding neighbors moved out, then you could possibly have the entire bird population in the area at your bird feeders! Most songbirds have a one to two-mile radius and will jump daily from feeder to feeder (and from yard to yard) within that radius. Birds are definitely creatures of habit. Their daily activities, such as sleeping, eating, bathing and preening, are done at the same time each day for the same length of time.

Each day that a bird says alive can be a minor miracle. Considering that they must be constantly on the lookout for overhead and ground predators, every hour can be trying. They must search for enough food and water each day and compete with others for the same. They must also find ways to remain warm and safe every night.

Again I say, it is amazing that they are able to survive at all.

So very cute

I took a short walk through the woods today and every once in awhile, I am reminded why I love nature and the birds so much. Just when you think you can't be surprised anymore, that's when they surprise you.

I had intended only a short walk, just about 50 feet back to check the trail camera. As I stepped into the pines, I heard nuthatches "yanking" in the treetops. Not just one, or two, but what seemed like a dozen of them. I looked up to see if I could spot them but they were invisible in the pine needles above me. They sounded like they were talking to each other, but that none of them was listening, just yakking. I found it unusual because I had only ever heard one or two nuthatches at a time.

It couldn't be that they were sounding the alarm about me - could it? I was reminded of blue jays and how they always put out the "danger" call when a predator is nearby. Once one jay took up the cry, they all started calling out.

This was similar but it surely couldn't have anything to do with me, could it? I mean, it had been awhile since I had been in the woods, but not THAT long!

As I was glancing upwards to see what they could be hollering about, I noticed the chickadees. They were dancing around on the lower branches of the pines. Six or seven of them were "pipping" to one another and were all keeping an eye on me. I thought that I was imagining things, but when they started coming down the branches towards me, I knew I wasn't imagining anything.

They acted like they were curious - like I was a monkey in the zoo that they had come to visit. As I watched the chickadees bounced around, they got closer and closer and closer to me until they were only about two feet over my head. What the heck?!, I thought. Maybe they wanted to land on me? I stuck my arm up towards them. They were so cute as they tilted their heads from side to side looking at my arm. They actually looked like they were considering coming down to check it out! Then I realized how stupid I must be - I mean, they aren't trained raptors that will come down to land on my forearm - what was I thinking?

I put my arm down and continued to watch the chickadees. They were content to keep an eye on me and I noticed that the nuthatches were still making their little noises up in the treetops.

I guess I was just the subject of conversation for the afternoon!

Sleeping not-quite-so-soundly

When humans don't sleep we show obvious signs. We have dark bags under our eyes, are lethargic, and are not at the top of our game. How would you know if a bird didn't get enough sleep? I don't know about you, but they all look kinda similar to me. I wouldn't know a sleep-deprived bird if I saw one. And yet how do birds sleep? And where?

While doing a little research, I found out that all types of birds sleep a little differently. Most perching birds have a special tendon in their feet and legs that automatically contracts when they alight on a branch. This allows them to sleep in trees without falling off of the branches. It's like a locking mechanism, and only when they lift their weight up can they unlatch their feet.

The majority of birds don't catch a full eight hours of Z's like we do. Chickadees, for instance, open their eyes every few minutes to check for predators, as I'm sure that many sleeping birds do. Some will seek out the shelter of roosting boxes, nesting boxes, hollow trees, snags, and bushes to cuddle up in, sometimes in large groups. Up to 15 male eastern bluebirds have been seen huddling in one nesting box to stay warm.

Other birds are solitary sleepers, huddling up next to tree trunks, in the crotch of a tree, or nestling deep within pine boughs to sleep.

Mourning doves seem to sleep almost anywhere where they can catch a few of the sun's rays and they will usually huddle up in small groups or three or four. Crows will fly as far as 30 miles to gather every evening and all roost together. Some of these "murders" of crows have from several hundred to a thousand individual birds.

If you've ever wondered where the birds sleep at night, all you have to do is wander through wooded areas just after twilight when the birds are settling in for the night. You can also watch them when they leave your feeders in the evening to see where they head. Sometimes you can hear them softly cheeping - probably reporting your position to one another. There have been many

Great Gray Owl

times when I've had sleeping grouse burst out from the pine trees overhead - usually scaring a few years off my life in the process.

It seems like it would be bad enough to have to look out for predators all the time, then there is also the weather that birds have to contend with. How do they ever make it through the night, and why don't they have bags under their eyes?

Observations

Thumper

• From Merrie N. of Sault Ste. Marie, *"Pelicans, I can't hardly believe it. Went to Mackinac Island today. Saw a big flock of cormorants. I had evening grosbeaks in the backyard, and I believe there is a grouse or a pheasant or something in the back woods. He is thumping like a small motorcycle taking off. What do you think it is? Also I keep hearing the nicest songbird, but haven't seen it yet. My neighbor says he thinks it is a white-crowned sparrow. Do they have a really nice song? I saw a charcoal gray and white bird (bigger than a robin). Do you think it is an Eastern Kingbird?"*

Clean Up Crew

• From Daryl F. of Sault Ste. Marie, *"Some bird observations: On our flowering crabapple fruit: partridge scarf them down whole, while grosbeaks tear them apart and the robin, if any are left by springtime, seem to do a combination. On our sunflower seed feeders: chickadees and nuthatches will carefully select a single seed to carry off and shuck while the goldfinches and purple finches stand in/on the feeder and shuck until stuffed.*

Our 'ground clean-up crew' will include morning doves and a pair of mallard ducks and they will scarf up anything not tied down. Other ground feeders include the juncos and all those what do you call them, lbjs (little brown jobbies), and they all shuck the seeds one at a time.

On the mallards, we have been having a pair around the property every spring for about ten years now. The odds would be against it being the same pair all these years, but never the less, just one pair. Yesterday morning the hen appeared with 13 young ones in tow, little balls of fluff and I am sure they were newly hatched. She didn't stay too long, but again last night she was back with her brood. After eating she made off with them in procession, through the dry culvert under the roadway and to the River."

Mystery Bands

• From Rudy of Barbeau, *"I am at a loss to know why I am over-populated with cow birds with bands. I thought these were for the purpose of cleaning up on cow dung? Are we expecting an infiltration of wild cows? Ha."*

Gray Catbird

Mystery Bird

• From Al D. of Brimley, *"As I am a casual birder I am able to identify a fair number of birds but I seldom will go very far out of my way to track a bird voice down to I.D. it. However, ... right in a thicket in my own yard as I step outside to enjoy my first hot cup of coffee in the early morning, I am inundated with a very vigorous and melodious singing fool of a bird. This is one secretive bird. I have inched my way close to the singer and it shuts up or flies away. I have gotten one fleeting look and the only thing I can match it to in my old Peterson guide is the Cat bird. Now I have never encountered one up here, only in Indiana decades ago. Since I am not a Birder I really do not get a lot of chances to check out our local bird population unless it flies into my view while I am outdoors fishing or hiking. But this is one frustrating bird. It does not limit its really beautiful singing to just the early morning hours. I now find myself running over to the thicket with binocs trying to get a full look at my mystery bird. It must have a nest in that thicket but I do not want to get in there and disturb the nesting area."*

Bitterly cold owl watching

One brutally cold winter, a friend of ours named Joe called us up and told us that he had found an empty field over near Fiber where he had seen short-eared owls hunting. Wow - this was great news because many of us had never seen a short-eared owl! Pat and I immediately drove over there and we were able to spy a few owls sitting on fence posts and occasionally flying over the field. Every time we drove there over the course of a week the wind was always blowing hard and the temperature was always below zero. We never wanted to get out of the car, the cold wind was so bad! Of course, I love to take photographs, but admit to NOT being a die-hard photo fan - I mean, I have my limits as to what I will endure for a good shot.

We called up a friend named Larry who was a professional wildlife photographer, and he buzzed up from Grand Haven for a weekend of possible great photo opportunities. We bundled up in just about every warm piece of clothing we had and headed over to the fields. The wind was still blowing and the air was so cold that everything on our vehicle was popping and groaning.

For some strange reason, the short-eared owls seemed to thrive in the cold. They were actively hunting in the late afternoon and ignored the bite of the wind as it fluffed their feathers and buffeted them around in the air. They were constantly on the lookout from their fence posts - scanning the fields for signs of mice and voles. Every now and then one would take off and go try its luck. The snow was not too deep yet, and it made hunting easier for the owls. It also made great photo opportunities for us.

About five or six people were there at the fields and everyone had binoculars up to their faces trying to get better views. The trouble was, everyone was so bundled up that it was hard to tell who was who! We knew most of the bird-watchers there, but a few were new faces.

Larry dragged his equipment out and set up a tripod and camera with a long zoom lens (and I mean REALLY long!). Focusing on a moving object is hard enough, but try doing it with heavy winter gloves on and it takes on a whole new dimension. And you did NOT dare to take off your gloves - it would have been almost instant frostbite. Pat and I shuffled around on the roadway talking to different people while Larry worked on getting some photographs. We tried to talk to one another, but our faces were frozen! The men with mustaches and beards had icicles and frost hanging from them and the rest of us could hardly move our mouths. We would try to say something and it would come out all mangled, almost like we were first learning to talk! The more we tried to talk and couldn't, the funnier it got. Our eyes felt like they were being frozen and we found yourself squinting a lot and sheltering our eyes from the wind. It was brutal out there - and yet the short-ears found a way to make it work for them.

They did not get a mouse every time they headed out to hunt, but their odds were pretty good. More often than not, they dove down with their feet to pull up something black and wiggling. Then they flew to the posts to swallow it whole.

We knew we could always get back in the cars to warm up if we needed to, and we did it often. Before we knew it, dusk had fallen and it had gotten too dark to see anymore. We then left the owls to do their hunting in peace and we retreated.

70 miles-per-hour birding

When Pat and I travel, we participate in what we call "high-speed birding" or sometimes we call it "70-mph birding." It takes a special kind of eye to observe birds that quickly and often we are unsuccessful in our efforts. Usually we can get the species correct, but not the specific kind of coloring of bird. This can lead to some heated discussions, all at 70 miles-per-hour, of course.

When we go birding on the side roads, we have the liberty to pull over to the side and check out the birds more carefully, but not so when we are on the expressway.

Expressway bird-watching is a challenge, to say the least. You cannot easily pull over, nor is it legal to do so.

It's more like, "Did you see that?"

"See what?"

"That bird in that tree by the road... it's too late now, we're way past it."

It is challenging and when both people see the bird ahead in the distance and are both able to see it, it is fun to share the sighting. That can lead to a discussion about that particular bird, what it is doing, if we've seen any there in the past, and if we might possibly see one there again.

You can make road lists if you like and engage in a friendly competition to see who can spot the most species of birds - that helps to pass the time. Or you can see who can spot the birds first. Each person in the vehicle has an advantage. The driver has the advantage where he is always looking ahead and can scan the roadsides ahead and to the front. The passenger has the advantage where he can look to whatever side he wants, or even backward if he wants. So, as you see, the game is equal among the participants.

Sure, it is easy to just put the car in "drive" and let it do its thing while you zone out to some tunes going down the highway.

But it is MUCH more interesting if you pay attention along the way and notice your surroundings. You will be amazed at how fast the time in the vehicle goes by. And, you just might win the contest!

Birds are everywhere

There's something about birds that is universal. If you get one person talking to another about birds, then there is often at least one other person that will join in the conversation.

If you think about it, has there been any time in your life when you have been outside where there has NOT been the presence of at least one bird? Any time we do something outdoors, there almost has to be birds. Think about it.

If you are at a sports event, even if it is in a sports dome, aren't there birds around you? Maybe gulls cleaning up the remains of the food around the area? Or maybe pigeons bopping around on the pavement looking for scraps too? Are they there and you just aren't aware of them? I'll bet that there is a bird somewhere nearby, either on a rooftop, or in a nearby tree or perhaps just flying overhead.

Birds inundate our lives, whether we realize it or not. Even the most obtuse person in the country can probably relate a bird story to you. Perhaps you were walking along minding your own business when bird poo came out of the sky and baptized you. Perhaps you were having a picnic at the park and a plump pigeon sat on a nearby post watching and waiting for some leftover crumbs. Perhaps you were at the beach having a sandwich and you looked away for only a moment and a gull swiped one of your potato chips? These are events that we soon forget and brush aside.

Once you pay attention - even if you are not a bird-watcher - you will notice that birds are literally everywhere. Kind of neat when you think about it. Having wings allows a bird to go where it wants and when it wants. That makes them able to "drop in" on you anytime you are outside. Now that you know - good luck not picturing that target on the top of your head the next time you go outside.

Chapter Four

Red-breasted Nuthatch

Lovely red-breasted nuthatches

There is something about those little red-breasted nuthatches. I just love them. They are so cute, and daring and shy that they have taken my heart. I like to watch them when they buzz into the bird feeders and then buzz back out again. They don't bother anybody, they don't annoy any of the other birds at the bird feeder, they just come in, grab a seed or two, and leave.

If you watch them, you can see how they zip over to one of the nearest trees, then spend a few minutes running down the trunk in a spiral motion. They look for nooks and crannies to jam seeds into, or possibly to find some treats for themselves that they left there earlier.

One day I had something neat happen. The husband and I were walking down a trail through a pine forest when I felt a slight breeze blow by my face.

There, not two feet from me, sat a red-breasted nuthatch. It was perched on a bare branch in a Scotch Pine and was gazing at me intently. I stood still and giddily watched it from such a close distance that I was thrilled inside. It just sat there for maybe six seconds regarding me calmly, then it went "yank!" and flew away.

Wow - I felt really special. Not only was I able to see one from so close, but it actually looked at me! It's hard to look into the eyes of a bird - they are a bottomless black that you can lose yourself into, and yet you never seem to touch their soul.

Still, it was an experience for me to remember. Did the nuthatch remember me? Doubtful that it even remembered seeing me five minutes later. Such is life.

The great god woodpecker

Often when I walk amid our stand of Northern Michigan woods, I can hear a distant "wuk-wuk-wuk" echoing through the forest.

That call from far overhead always reminds me of a monkey in a South American rainforest.

In the past, I have come upon a large dead tree trunk and have seen wood chips and long strips of bark flying through the air. This is the work of a pileated woodpecker at his job. A huge pile of wood pieces accumulates quickly at the base of the tree as his slow, rhythmic thunking continues. Occasionally, he cocks his head to the side as if listening for the pitter-patter of a juicy wood-boring beetle under his feet. Due to his large size and big, brave demeanor, he was not afraid of me as I slowly crept up on him.

Suddenly, WHACK! He pulls out a wiggly larvae, swallows it whole, and flies off - all in one motion. That was the Great God Woodpecker in action.

The pileateds have had many colorful names throughout history. Usually the name stems from a person's initial reaction at seeing them. One common name is Log Cock, or Wood Kate. Also common is Lord God woodpecker or Good God woodpecker. In actuality, the word pileated means having a crest covering the pileum, and a pileum is the top of a bird's head from the bill to the nape of the neck.

To me, this particular woodpecker reminds me of the old Woody Woodpecker cartoons that I used to watch as a child. I can almost hear Woody's laughter in the background - can you?

Pileated Woodpeckers

Quirky behaviors

There are lots of bird behaviors that happen every second of the day that we just plain never see. We are too busy with our own lives to pay attention to birds all of the time. We think we have quirky behaviors - well let me tell you, we have got nothing to compare with some of the things that birds do on a daily basis. I truly believe that birds have a sense of humor at times - maybe not on purpose, but it seems to be there.

Pet Crow

Daryl F. shares some of these strange behaviors with us: *"When I was a freshman in high school I took a crow before it could fly and kept it for a pet until that fall. It used to get food from the dog's dish and when the dog came after it, it would hop away sideways and hold one wing up like it was fending the dog off. Like we would raise an arm to protect from a blow. I think it was playing with the dog or teasing it. No matter how fast or slow the dog came after it the crow would stay just out of reach and stop exactly at the end of the chain and sit (stand) and look at him. Of course the dog would turn around and go back to his house as if he had done his duty.*

The robin that had a nest in the spruce tree beside our driveway had a worm in its beak and squatted down in the driveway dirt and pulled its version of the broken winged killdeer. A red squirrel dashed out of the bush and after the robin but of course the robin flew the coop. That was the first time I've seen something other than a killdeer do that.

Nature is kind to us and entertaining if we only notice."

Facts about feathers

We have got hair and they have got feathers. When we are discussing why birds can fly and we can't, that seems to be the key element.

Man has been intrigued with birds for thousands of years. We can swim like fish, jump like rabbits, run like deer, and climb like a squirrel, but no matter how hard we try, we just cannot fly like a bird. I am reminded of the legend of the guy who glued feathers to his body and attempted to fly to the sun - yes, it was only a legend, and no, it's not possible. We are too heavy and our bones are far from hollow.

Birds are the only living creatures in our world with feathers. The feathers constitute roughly one-third of a songbird's total body weight.

One exception is the frigatebird, who is outweighed by its own feathers. Just as everything in life is proportional and some humans are hairier than others, so it is that some birds have more feathers than others. Think of a frigatebird as that big, hairy-backed man you know who has hair coming out of his t-shirt at the chest and out his ears and nose.

The total number of feathers a bird has varies from bird to bird, but it does roughly correlate to their body size. A hummingbird, for instance, has about 1,000 feathers, whereas a swan can have over 20,000 feathers.

Feathers are crucial to a bird's very existence and their maintenance is an important part of every bird's daily routine. It is absolutely vital that birds keep their plumage in tip-top condition. A specific part of each bird's day is spent cleaning and re-arranging their feathers.

Birds preen by gently tucking in and stroking each feather with their bill - zipping up any splits. Preening also removes parasites and dirt, and arranges feathers into position. Every now and then, the bird squeezes its bill against the preen gland (under the tail) to collect preen oil. Its bill then spreads this oil in a thin film over the feathers. The parts of the body, such as the head, that the bird can't reach are oiled by rubbing against previously oiled parts, or by scratching with the feet.

The preen oil kills bacteria and fungi and helps to lubricate the feathers so they don't become brittle and break off. Studies have shown that a bird who has been prevented from oiling becomes scruffy and can't fly as effectively.

When feathers are damaged or lost, the bird's insulation is severely compromised and their flight becomes more strenuous. The air trapped between the feathers can help the bird keep out wind and repel rain. In a cold Upper Peninsula winter, this loss of insulation can cost the birds their lives.

At other times, when a bird is being pursued by a predator, even a slight flight disadvantage can spell disaster. A bird needs to be at its best at all times, and feather maintenance is a must in their routine.

Damaged feathers are usually replaced once or twice a year by a process called molting. Molting is when a bird renews all or part of its plumage by shedding old or worn-out feathers and growing new ones.

Many times when you see a weird-looking bird, like it's kind of mottled - that's when a bird is shedding/molting. Some birds will disappear entirely when they are molting and then magically reappear with new feathers. Others seem like they gradually turn into different colors.

Favorite birds - once more

Again, why do we favor certain birds over others? It makes no sense, yet I find myself falling into the same school of thought as many of my birding friends.

I admit that I would rather see a little chickadee over a fat, ugly starling. See? There it comes out, right there. Even how I describe the birds announces my feelings for them. I am not immune to bird favoritism, it seems.

Swallow Meals

Tom P. from Sault Ste. Marie describes a scene where he felt similarly: *"I witnessed an event while fishing behind the Edison Sault Powerhouse (a water dam building between a canal and the St. Marys River). We had our boat tied up at the back of the powerhouse so that we could fish securely without drifting away into the river. Two young cliff swallows (they nest on the back wall of the powerhouse) flew out of their nest and directly into the current of the river. About the time we thought we should untie and try to get them with a landing net, the gulls had already taken care of them. Two more met a similar fate later. There's just a short piece of grass back there where the birds can land after taking their first flight. I wonder how many of them actually make it to adulthood back there? Doesn't seem like the odds are very good, but I guess some of them must make it.*

It's funny how one particular species can affect you more than anoth-er. I worried about the cute, fuzzy swallows, yet I'm not sure it would have bothered me to watch a young herring gull get picked off by a marsh hawk or northern pike! The darn gulls picked off the killdeer, too, shortly after they hatched at our cabin down in Barbeau."

Pigeon Pests

Joanne S. from Sault Ste. Marie describes her favorite birds a different way: *"We live on Riverside Drive on the river near 3 Mile and are having some luck attracting mostly chickadees, hairy woodpeckers, mourning doves, goldfinches, sparrows . . . and pigeons. Whole bunches of pigeons who eat most of the feed we put out. Do you have any sugges-tions for discouraging these pests? They clean out all kinds of feeders: tubes, platforms, enclosed houses with trays, it doesn't seem to matter. I guess the thistle seed is the only thing they leave alone."*

Crabby mom

One day, while driving down our dirt road, I spied a sandhill crane standing on the edge of the road. As I got closer, she moved away from the edge of the road. The grass there was about a foot high, but it was sparse in places. By the time I arrived at where she had been standing and came to a stop, she was now eight or nine feet off the road standing in the grass. She stood there like a statue and calmly watched me. I wondered what she was doing when all of a sudden she started to holler. A sandhill crane's voice from that

Sandhill Cranes

proximity was deafening and I couldn't figure out why she was upset.

And then I saw them. Two little soft yellow fuzzballs with long legs were creeping around in the grass struggling to head to her side. As they passed through the no-grass areas, I could see them for a brief second. They were cute!

At that moment I heard a second crane start to cry out. For a second or two, I couldn't figure out where the noise was coming from, then I caught a movement in my rear-view mirror. There, standing behind the truck, was Poppa Sandhill. It seemed that the two adults were communicating to each other, and I'm sure that it was about me.

I looked back at Momma and she gave me what I am sure was a dirty look. She reached down into the grass and started yanking up beakfuls of grass. Then she tossed it into the air in my direction. Yank-toss, yank-toss, yank-toss. I could tell she was really getting agitated. By now the chicks had already reached where she was at and they were heading into deeper grass behind her.

Then I heard Poppa cry out again, only he had flown over the truck and was standing in front of me on the road. He stalked up to the truck with an air of surety, and then, as if leading me, turned around and started walking up the road. When he got about 15 feet away, he dropped one of his wings down to the ground and

Sandhill Crane

started hollering again. I'll be darned, he was pulling the old bro-ken-wing act! Down the road he went, drawing my attention away from those precious little fuzzballs in the grass.

I admit - I was distracted! So rather than keep on getting them all worked up, I obliged by starting to drive away slowly down the road towards Poppa. After I was well beyond where the Momma and babies were at, then Poppa's wing suddenly got better and he flew off of the road.

I had been able to witness one of nature's defense techniques first hand that day. It's a good thing that Poppa distracted me, because I am pretty sure that that grass-throwing would not have worked.

A pet peeve

We all have them... pet peeves. My pet peeve originates from an actual incident (or maybe two). I absolutely can't stand it when people who make bird houses put perches on the front of them. To me, they are totally uneducated as far as birds go and they are making a grave error.

Do many of these bird-house makers know this? Probably not, but I sure try to tell them when I can. As makers of bird houses ourselves, we know how easy it is to put a perch on a bird house, and also that it tends to make the house 'cuter.' It seems to add a finishing touch and completes the project.

I am here to tell you - don't do it! And don't buy a bird house unless you can take off the perch.

Part of this pet peeve comes from a few incidents I have observed. Let me tell you about one...

Pat and I had put up a little bluebird house in our front yard and there was a predator guard on the front of it over the entrance hole. What we didn't realize is that the predator guard - which is meant to keep out squirrels and raccoons - is the perfect place for a predatory bird to perch.

We watched in delight as tree swallows took over the bird house and started hauling in nesting materials. They flew back and forth for days with various types of dry grasses and weeds.

Tree Swallows

We knew they were just about done when they ended up with feathers in their beaks one day. They took the feathers inside and lined the interior of the nest with a nice, soft lining for the chicks to-come.

Momma tree swallow spent what seemed like an inordinate amount of time laying eggs and then hatching them. Every few days we would peek inside the box to see her progress. She never acted like she minded and we never overstayed our welcome.

Finally the eggs hatched and we celebrated. Yay! Four chicks are here! Both parents started the arduous process of catching bugs and grubs and hauling them into the nesting box. All day long they both would do this - over and over and over again. They would rest briefly on the edge of the predator guard with the bug, then realign it and scoot inside. As the chicks grew and started to grow feathers, they started to climb up to the nest box hole and take turns waiting for their parents to bring them food. Once they got a treat, they would fall back to the nest and a sibling would take their place. It was cute seeing their little faces in the dark hole of the nest box.

One day I glanced at the bird house from inside the house and saw something unusual. There was a DIFFERENT bird perched on the front of the bird house. What was it? I grabbed up the binoculars and checked it out. Uh oh. There was a kestrel conveniently perched on the front of the bird house, hanging on to the predator guard (they can ALSO hang onto the perches). As I watched in horror, the kestrel waited for a chick to come up to the hole then it grabbed it! The kestrel pulled the chick out of the hole by its head, then it opened up its wings and flew away with it. I couldn't believe my eyes.

One by one, that kestrel came back and unloaded that nest box, taking each nestling away to feed its own hungry young somewhere. Then, when a parent tree swallow went inside to see where the chicks were, the kestrel landed one last time and grabbed up the parent too!

Once you see something like this, you develop a distaste for perches on bird houses. See if you forget this story the next time you see a bird house for sale with a perch on the front of it.

Mysterious birds in mysterious places

One day I was contacted by Bill R. from the Sault. He mentioned that he had some interesting bird stories he wanted to share. One of them involved a dead bird.

Bill has a through-the-wall fireplace (with a round smokestack) in his house which is visible from two rooms. One day last summer he was cleaning out the ashes in the bottom of the fireplace. He reached up and opened the flue and a few dead flies fell out.

He glanced up and there seemed to be something stuck in the fireplace flue. A second later, a hen merganser fell out also. It was apparent that it had gotten down into the round chimney somehow (why would it want to? maybe the warmth?) and had gotten down to the diversion plate and was trapped. Bill said the interesting thing was that it had never made any noise at all and that it had to get by the damper first to get where it was. He couldn't figure it out, nor could I.

Hummingbirds fly south in more than one way

There was an interesting conversation one day at a family gathering we attended. It had to do with hummingbirds. This was a topic that I had heard more than once and it amazed me that it was still traveling through the 'grapevine.'

I was asked by a sister-in-law if the hummingbirds had made it back from down south yet. "You know they ride on the backs of geese, right?", she said. Well, my amazement must have given itself away when my mouth dropped open and hung there. "Noooo, they do not," I said. "Oh yes, they do. I've known that for years. It's the only way they're able to fly such long distances!"

It was hard to argue with a logic like that that had been cemented in her mind for so many years. The truth of the matter is NO, hummingbirds do NOT ride on the backs of geese or any other sort of bird when they migrate. This lady had it all figured out and it made perfect sense to her. The only way I could disprove it (as she wouldn't believe me if I just plain said so) was to show her facts and figures.

Apparently, this rumor began to circulate in the 1800s when a bird professional was playing a practical joke on a friend. The ornithologist was also an avid bird hunter. One day he found a dead hummingbird on his lawn and he tucked it into the body feathers of a Canada goose that he had had mounted and stuffed.

The next time his friend came to visit, he showed him the hummingbird in the feathers and said, "See, that's just how I found the hummingbird when I shot the goose!" Of course, the friend believed him because his friend was so knowledgeable about birds, he must know what he's talking about. And, of course, he spread the word from there.

The truth and the scientific evidence tells us two things. First of all, hummingbirds and geese travel to two totally different parts of the world when they migrate so NO, they would not carpool, not even partway.

Second of all, when geese and hummingbirds migrate, they fly

Canada Goose

Ruby-throated Hummingbird

at different altitudes. A hummingbird has to stop occasionally to refuel, as it is such a small bird - while geese fly at high altitudes and very seldom stop to eat along the way.

Now, having said all that, an interesting newspaper article was sent to me by Lois L. in Sault Ste. Marie. The *Tampa Tribune* featured an article in 1999 about a hummingbird that got the chance to travel by jet!

It seems the ruby-throated hummingbird had been eating sugar water at a bar not far from Green Bay, WI when it collapsed to the ground. The bar patrons rushed outside to grab up their cute little friend and they took it to a wildlife rehabilitator, who determined that the early snap of cold weather they had had wilted all of the hummingbird's main food sources. She proceeded to bring the hummingbird back to health and by then, it had missed its normal migration.

The rehabber, in turn, teamed up with a rehabber from Florida, who would release the hummingbird down south. In the meantime, a woman named Bonnie Vaughn agreed to take the bird along with her as carry-on luggage on her own flight to Florida. Airline officials originally balked at letting a bird on board, but eventually relented. The hummingbird had to be fed every 10 to 15 minutes on the flight and successfully flew the 1,303 miles to Florida - with the help of a few friends.

Now that's a true story of a hummingbird riding on the back (or inside) of a much larger bird.

Chapter Five

Common birds

Many of my stories feature certain birds over and over again. I would apologize, except that I am not sorry! Birds like turkeys, mourning doves, chickadees, grouse, hummingbirds, and tree swallows are common in our area, so it would make sense that I have had a lot of experience in watching them.

What I have found instead is that even the so-called "common" birds that we observe every day have something to teach us. Their daily behaviors can be amazing, at times. It is many of these behaviors that you will read about in chapters to follow.

Hummingbirds are one bird that I never tire of watching. There is something fascinating about those tiny creatures that can do such amazing things. They are the only bird that can fly backwards and even upside-down and their aerial feats are astounding to watch. In fact, many times as I watch them fly, it's hard to believe they are doing what they are doing - even while I'm watching them do it!

So, naturally, there will be a few hummingbird stories in this book, as I love the little squirts and all their antics.

One morning we were sitting out on the deck in our Adirondack chairs. We were soaking in the beauty of the morning before we headed out to our various tasks. Zooooooooooom! There went a hummingbird right in front of us. Zooooooooooom! There went a hummingbird right behind us. I had forgotten that we were sitting between two liquid hummingbird feeders which were about 50 feet apart. As a hummer flies, that would be about one second, or so it seemed.

That morning there was a territorial dispute going on. It was a fact that a hummingbird sitting on one of the feeders could see a hummingbird land on the other feeder. And so the chase began. Every time one would spy the other, it would zoom off to chase it away. In the meantime, another hummingbird would fly in from the woods and sneak a drink from the one he had just left. So then he would zoom back to chase off the interloper. Then the first sneak was back and he would zip back to the first bird feeder. And so it went, back and forth every minute or so.

Ruby-throated Hummingbird

It was all very tiring to watch - I don't know how they did it so much. I guess you could say that hunger was a factor. Rumor has it that if you see two hummingbirds, then you actually have four times that amount - or eight hummingbirds.

After awhile of watching this, I knew we had been sitting there too long when the hummers started ignoring us and treating us like furniture. On one pass, the hummingbird flew so close to my head that it parted my hair in a new place! Now if that doesn't make you duck, I don't know what will!

Feather zipping

The feather itself - what a remarkable instrument. Not only is it light, but it is also strong and flexible. Feathers are grown out of keratin, the same substance that we humans use to grow fingernails and hair. One wonders why we can't teach ourselves how to grow feathers instead of body hair. Think of all the fashion and new personal accessories that would spring out of that!

An individual feather can be compared to a zipper or to a piece of velcro - both manmade objects that probably used feathers for inspiration. Tiny hooks off of the individual parts of the feather are used in a complex manner to hold the whole structure together. Without boring you with the details and all of the technical terms, basically we can say that a feather derives its strength from the way that the little hooks hold onto one another.

A bird can use its bill to repair damaged feathers by nibbling them or by running its bill along the feathers' length to "zip" up those hooks or barbs. It instinctively knows that its feathers are life-sustaining and that damaged feathers mean its demise.

When a bird's feathers get too worn or damaged for repair, then it simply molts off the bad feathers and grows new ones.

So how does one go about growing a feather? It can't come out of the skin fully formed - how prickly would that be?

This is how it happens:

1) The old feather falls away.

2) The new feather shaft starts to grow, resembling a plastic drinking straw.

3) Within the shaft, the feather is developing barbs crammed into a tightly packed spiral.

4) After awhile, the tip of the shaft splits, allowing the feather to unfold like a fan into its final shape.

So how does a bird grow all of the different types of feathers that it has on its body? Body contour feathers look unlike wing or tail feathers and the down feathers underneath are also unique.

It must be something in the genetics, because I am sure a bird does not grow specific feathers by its own will alone, but because nature knows somehow that it needs them. Now if we could only figure out how to do that!

A peeping tom

One day while Pat and I were having a calm afternoon of relaxation in our living room, we had an unusual event happen.

Our living room windows are large and wide, and they sit low to the ground, maybe two feet up on the outside and maybe six inches up on the inside of the house. They are perfect for bird watching and even the cat (Pheebee) likes to recline with her front paws curled up on the windowsill to watch the birds in the backyard.

Pat and I were reading, each lost in our own world of either news or fiction, when he quickly glanced up and over to the windows. "What is it?!", I said. "I don't know, I thought I saw something," he said to me.

There was nothing out there that we could see, so after a moment's thought, we both turned back to our individual reading.

A few minutes later, Pat looked up again and turned towards the windows. "I swear I could have seen something out of the corner of my eye," he said. "Well, I sure don't even see anything moving out there," I replied. We both continued to look outside and when we were again convinced that nothing was around, we again went back to bury our noses in our books.

A few seconds later the cat went zipping by towards the windows at a fast gallop and just about crashed into the glass! It seemed that she had seen something too! Now Pat and I were even more curious and we couldn't stand it anymore - we had to get up and go to the windows and look outside.

Just as we approached the window, an ugly, naked red head popped up over the windowsill and peered in at us. Wow - what a shock - that was a wild turkey! Pheebee chose that moment to exert her considerable feline authority in the household. She jumped up from her spot next to the window and tapped the glass with her paws like she was going to jump through the window!

The turkey just about came unglued! What was that awful black-and-white creature on the other side of that glass that was coming at it?! It jumped up with a frightened look on its face, flapped its giant wings up once, and then turned tail and took off running away from the house. Its long legs carried it through the

Wild Turkey

flower beds and across the short grass of the backyard in no time at all.

Pat and I sat there, shocked. It all happened so fast. We then took a look at Pheebee and started laughing. She was nonchalantly sitting next to the window washing her paw like nothing had happened.

It only took us a quick second to piece it all together... the turkey had been walking next to the house looking for bugs and errant seeds. Every now and then it had poked its head up to look around for danger.

The turkey was just tall enough that when it stood next to the window it could look into the house with ease. And yet when we glanced over at it, it already had its head back down close to the ground looking for more food.

You could say that it was a true "peeping tom."

Observations

There are many times when the readers of my column have had a wonderful way with words. They would think of ways to describe the birds that they were seeing which were far better than any ways that I could ever have described them:

Shrike Intrigue

Amy K. wrote: *"In January we observed a northern shrike at our feeder chasing a chickadee one day and a goldfinch the next day. All the little birds would be gone and the shrike would dart from spot to spot until a new bird came in to feed and then the chase was on. Both times that we watched, the smaller bird got away but not until the two birds circled many times until they got to a dense wooded area. We enjoyed this show out our window while we had dinner about 5:00 that evening. It was tense for a while, but we liked the happy ending!"*

Waterfront Fun

Helen S. from Les Cheneaux wrote: *"My daughter, Joanna, lives in Cedarville. This week she had three - one male and two female - cardinals at her feeder and I watched the antics of two huge pileated woodpeckers at our feeder. We also often see eagles and a pair of ospreys that we enjoy watching each spring. We enjoy watching the waterfowl there as well."*

Lord God Woodpecker

Al D. from Brimley wrote: *"Had a first for me yesterday. We have always had pileateds come to our suet. But yesterday a male (??) came to the base of a large balsam and actually cleared away the snow, about 18 inches, and started hammering away at the base.*

Did this for a solid TWO hours. I observed for the first 30 minutes but then gave it up to do other things but I checked every now and then. Then today I came home from town and while I was unloading it flew to the base again and started the routine again.

Nothing seems to bother it. My wife walked past it. I inched to within 15 feet to get some pics with my 300 tele. Tricky, as it kept bobbing its head out of sight and then back above the snow.

Have any number of trees with big neat holes from this activity but have never observed this. I am guessing it must be large ants. We have had several trees blow over and I had to cut one last summer and all had a colony of very large ants in the base.

It is neat to watch this bird - he is very determined. Tree pieces are flying all over the snow. The light is such that I got a good close look into a big cavity, elongated, that it has carved and there ARE tunnels just like the ones in my fallen trees that contained the large ants. I'm going to keep observing this."

Switching Places

Helen B. from the Soo wrote: *"We don't get the paper but my mother saves the Sunday paper for me to read all your articles! I live in the Sault and have recently gotten bitten by the bird watching bug!*

We get chickadees, nuthatches, wrens, sparrows and such... my most exciting thing I must report to you is that I have both a pair of hairy and a pair of downy woodpeckers that visit my suet on a regular basis. I have so much fun watching and journaling them!

First the male will come then the female. They seem to switch off and on as if to say...'Hey honey, isn't it your turn to go get the food for the family today?!' "

Goshawk vs. squirrel

One of the raptors that we occasionally have hanging around our house is a goshawk. Now, if you know anything at all about these birds, they are silent and majestic and they always seem to appear out of nowhere. We have blamed them for the disappearance of our ruffed grouse and our occasional pheasant, as we know they are large and fierce enough to take either one.

For all of their large size, the goshawk is still a fearsome predator and is extremely agile and skilled at flight through the woods. There have been many times when we have seen one zipping through the woods like an errant bomber on a suicide mission. Other times, a goshawk will suddenly dip down over the top of our house and scare the living daylights out of all the birds feeding at the bird feeders in the backyard. The bluejays start screaming, the chickadees and goldfinches dart for cover, and all the other birds who were caught unawares pretend that they are statues.

The weird thing is that I don't think they are agile enough to go after the littler birds, but they still like to put the predator fear into them from time to time.

One day we saw something odd happening in the woods behind our house. We kept seeing a flash of gray appear through the trees near the ground. Pat and I crowded up near the windows and tried to get a better look. From underneath a low-hanging pine tree a goshawk walked out. It appeared that it had its eye on a dead red squirrel that was only a few feet from where it had been hiding. The goshawk kept glancing anxiously towards the house, almost like it knew we were there and we made it nervous.

The goshawk hopped up on top of the squirrel and seemed to squat down for a moment. Then it made a mighty hop, like it was going to fly away with the squirrel. There was only one problem, the squirrel was too heavy for it! Instead of a leap into the air, all that happened was that the rodent was moved about six inches. There was a rest, and then another hop was made. Then the hawk let go and jumped up and flew away.

A few minutes later the goshawk came back. It again repeated its activity - hopping and moving the squirrel a few inches at a time. We were not sure what its ultimate goal was, other than it didn't like where the squirrel was laying. Each time it would move it a foot or two, then fly away in what seemed like frustration.

After about four or five moving sequences, the hawk had the squirrel neatly tucked underneath a bush. Now it stopped moving around and got down to the business at hand. The hawk had decided that that squirrel was going to be its dinner, but it was NOT going to eat it out in the open where another predator could steal it out from under its talons. The whole hopping routine was all about going undercover!

That was a neat thing to see, and one that we were lucky to observe. A few minutes later that squirrel was hidden and we would never have noticed anything going on in the woods.

Bird identification - by email

Here we go again, maybe you can help me?

Kris G. from Sault Ste. Marie asks: *"I recently saw a huge, strange bird at our little, commercial suet feeder. I've never seen one like him before, nor since. He must have been at least 7+" long with a large body. I really don't know how to describe him except to say that he looked something like a gigantic sparrow with a very distinguishing feature different from a sparrow; he had an extremely long, narrow beak - almost needle-like and about 2" long. He stayed for a fair time eating away, but has never returned to my knowledge. Perhaps we were just a stopping off place for him on his way to more permanent headquarters. Though he was definitely thick through the body, it was at least partially due to the fact that his feathers were very 'fluffed up.' Oh, in being like a sparrow, he was shaded of brown. Do you have any idea what kind of bird he must be?*

When the weather is calm, we lift the lid on our 'indoor' feeder with the glass enclosure trying to tempt some birds to partake. However, we have only had one shortly after it was mounted who flew in for a feed. Today we have had only a squirrel sitting inside for a very long time; it's the first time a squirrel got in to our knowledge. He was almost as big as the inside of the feeder and I thought he couldn't get out because he'd eat for a time and then stick his head up sadly over the edge of the glass and stare at me. I asked my husband to get a plank or something to let him out of his predicament, but he just laughed and said, 'Just open the door to the deck and he'll get out.' I thought he just didn't want to brave the elements. Poor thing looked so stuck, I felt badly for him and a little provoked that my husband wouldn't help him out. I told him that I would take a ladder out for him and he said, 'You don't need a ladder - it'll just jump on you first!' Of course, this scared me off so I just kept checking on him. He continued to alternate between stuffing himself and looking sadly over the glass something like 'Kilroy was here.' The last time I looked, he had disappeared. I had just experienced the perfect squelch and felt fairly foolish for my wasted emotion."

Tom P. from Lake Superior State University writes: *"I wonder if you can help us I.D. some birds we've been seeing on the Lake State campus. They're robin-sized birds in groups of a dozen or more. They're always in fruit trees, usually eating in the small crabapple trees around here. They're brownish gray with an orange-rust-colored cap. The rust color extends down their backs, under the wings. The wings are the brownish-gray with a distinctive white stripe and it looks like a black stripe underneath it, if not above it, too.*

I believe in your column you mentioned pine grosbeaks being in the area. We looked up pine grosbeak in our bird books and it seems to be a close, but not exact fit. The books say the pine grosbeak has two white stripes on the wing or 'shoulder.' We see only one stripe, but maybe two show up in the bird's spring plumage? My book says the birds are tame and easily approachable. That fits these birds. I once went out the door, heard a peep and turned to see a dozen sitting in a small tree a few feet away from me. The have a very soft, short 'trill' for a voice. We saw two dozen or more in a grove of fruit trees by the president's house and they were sitting just a few feet above our heads, not concerned at all about our presence."

Love is in the air

Springtime is one of my favorite times of the year. Even though everything looks dirty for awhile, it isn't long before the new grass starts shooting up in the lawn and the trees open up their little green buds and they unfurl into leaves. Butterflies magically appear out of thin air - at least it seems that way - and flies begin to buzz you whenever you head outside.

Birds also can feel the pull of spring. With them it is more powerful than most creatures. They have already spent the last few weeks enraptured by a strong drive within their bodies to fly hundreds and/or thousands of miles. It is this same drive that leads them to perform their various mating dances and rituals.

Just as the variety of birds is numerous, so are the ways that the males choose to woo their little women. It doesn't matter if they mate for life, or if they choose a new partner every year, they still are driven to perform the age-old dance.

Some of these dances are subtle, like a few of the songbirds that sing beautifully and wiggle a few tail and wing feathers to attract a woman's attention.

Many others, however, are more energetic and creative. The ruffed grouse pretends that he is a mighty drummer - and indeed he is as he beats the heck out of deadfall logs with his wings in the springtime. It starts off as a slow, steady beat then steadily increases to a blur of sound before he finishes. And then a few minutes later it starts all over again.

The sandhill crane, being a much larger bird, believes that it must also perform a much larger display. It nods and bows towards the female, and if she seems interested then he will dance from side to side using his whole body and then finish up with a short little celebratory flap up into the air a few feet - hollering all the while. All in all, it's very impressive.

Whooping cranes couples will both get into the act. The male approaches the female and bows. Then both birds begin to simultaneously display - stepping, standing, and flapping in unison. At the end, sometimes the male will leap completely over the female.

Peacocks are another matter entirely. They grow these multicolor, multi-hued beautiful feathers all over their body and then grow an enormously long tail that the peahen couldn't ignore if she tried. And THEN the peacocks will also perform an elaborate dance in front of the female that shows off all of their best features.

The tiny hummingbird often tries to impress the drab female with his flying prowess. He zips by her as fast as he can, then turns back to do it again. When she is sitting still and he has what he thinks is her undivided attention, he will perform fantastically high U-shaped flying formations in front of her to try to get her attention.

Another bird that surprised me when I caught them was a rock dove (a pigeon!). A female was bobbing along on the ground looking for some small tidbits. She was successfully ignoring a male who was trying his best to make her pay attention. He was performing a series of fancy turns and figure-eights around her. He could have been a performer on television with his fancy footwork!

Wild Turkeys

Turkey doofus

For quite a few years, we had a small flock of about six wild turkeys that liked the trees to roost in our front yard every night. They were amusing and we always got a kick out of watching them every night around dusk when they would get ready to go up into the trees.

Now, I don't know how much you know about turkeys, but there are differing theories about them; they are really either very smart or very dumb. The jury is still out on this matter, and maybe by the end of reading this book, you'll be able to make your own decision one way or the other.

Anyway, every night just before dark the turkeys would wander over into our front yard and they would start to mill around, looking up into the treetops all the while. After a few minutes, one would take the lead. It would run about 10 steps across the grass, flapping all the while, and then would become airborne and fly up about 20 feet or so where it would crash land into the top branches of an elm or popple tree. It would scrabble around with its feet and beak until it was able to gain a purchase on a branch and it would then settle down its feathers.

The rest of the turkeys would then follow it, and each would land in a different tree, all close to the first turkey's tree. In the morning, close to first light, they would all leap off of their branch and glide down (or as close to a glide as a round-bodied bird like a turkey can do) to the grass of the front yard.

One day we awoke to hear a whole bunch of gobbling. A turkey could be heard over on the side of our house in the woods gobbling like crazy. When we went out to investigate, we found that a silly turkey had come down from its roost and had accidentally landed in our sewage lagoon! Well, not IN it, but on the side. The whole lagoon is about 20 feet across and is fenced in with a 4-foot fence. It has a few feet of edge all around the water where the turkey was currently running around and around.

It was trapped! Or so it thought. As we observed, the turkey would run the circle inside, gobbling in distress. At the same time, the rest of the flock would be running all along the outside of the fence "cooing" back at him. None of the turkeys could find a way out of the lagoon for their flock buddy.

Hello. Dummies. You can FLY out. This is a case for the turkey mentality being very LOW.

Pat tried to help the stupid thing. He would try to scare it on one side of the lagoon, which would make it take off flying across the water (and we hoped it would then fly right over the fence). Unfortunately, when it got to the side of the water, it would then land again - still INSIDE the fence.

No amount of prodding on our part - nor on the part of the other turkeys could convince this bird that he wasn't in mortal danger and that its fate lay in its own hands.

Finally, we gave up and left it to its own devices whether to get out or not. It was my theory that later that day, when it saw all of its buddies take off into the air to go roost in the trees, that it would get the same idea and fly right out of there.

Sure enough, the next morning the turkey was gone out of the lagoon. So you decide - dumb or smart?

You may not make it to adulthood

Suppose you and your spouse were thinking about starting a family. What if the doctor told you that there was only a 20 percent chance that your children would reach adulthood. Would you still consider it?

For a wild bird, there is nothing to think about. It is in their very nature to court, mate, and raise a brood or two each year. A bird's survival instincts are quite strong and it is that instinct which rules their every behavior.

The 20 percent survival rate is due to the horrendous problems birds face each nesting season. They deal with all kinds of nasty weather such as rain, hail, wind, and the hot sun. They also face predation from squirrels, snakes, raccoons, and even other birds.

Even against all these odds, wild birds have come up with many devious ways to increase their chances of success. Some will go so far as to build their nests close to an aggressive animal for protection.

Each species of bird makes a distinctive type of nest and there is a wide variation in the type of materials used. They employ everything from bare gravel and cinders to elaborate woven nests made from spider webs and lichen. Ornithologists tell us that the type of nest a bird builds is directly proportional to the degree of evolution that its species has achieved. The most advanced species of birds - like orioles and weaverbirds - have learned to wind, weave and tuck their nests together. The lesser advanced species - like grouse, turkeys or gulls - lay their eggs on gravel, rocks, or in the sand. Sometimes they just lay their eggs and hope for the best.

I have had a female killdeer who attempted to build a nest in our driveway one year. All she did was push aside a few small rocks and scoop out a hollow in the remaining dirt. She hopped around doing her broken-wing trick trying to lure us away from the site but we weren't fooled.

Killdeer

A few years ago, I had also observed a killdeer lay her eggs in a landscaped area filled with wood chips. Amazingly enough, in either environment killdeer eggs blend in very well and it is very difficult to tell where the nest is.

In general, though, most nests do protect the eggs to an extent and some will also protect the hatchlings.

The site of the nest also gives us a major clue to its owner. Usually a bird will use whatever materials are handy within its home feeding territory. The only exception may be seabirds. They hunt over water, so of course they would not want to build their nests in the water!

The variation of nests is amazing. Some nests are so tiny and so well camouflaged that even when the birds are incubating, you can't see the nest nor the bird! Others are so huge that the bird seems to be hidden inside. Hummingbirds will use spider webs to hold their tiny nests together, then gently decorate it with lichen on the outside, so that the nest looks just like a bump on the tree branch.

Orioles are one of the many kinds of birds who have learned to adapt to high winds. They build a sock-like nest high up in the trees and it is very deep so that the eggs won't swing or fall out. In the past when we have observed the female feeding the young, she dips right into the nest and you can't even see her!

All in all, we can say that nests are simply cradles for eggs. They can be a penguin's rocky cradle in the sand, or a dove's flimsy few twigs carelessly tossed together. Either way, they are home to many a brood and every year new nurseries are formed all around us.

Michigan babies

I cautiously walked across the yard, keeping one eye on the overhead sky, expecting to be "swooped" at any minute by one of our resident tree swallows.

Pat and I had been watching our line of bluebird houses for activity. We had noticed that chickadees were expressing interest in one of the houses. They had been zipping in and out of the entrance hole as if they were trying it on for size.

Then one day Pat noticed a chickadee entering the house with a bit of greenery in its beak. That was the day we decided to check out the inside of the boxes.

We approached the nest box and rapped lightly on the side to give anyone inside the chance to escape before we opened it up. No answer. Pat applied the screwdriver and in a few moments he had the clean-out door open.

I peered inside and was pleased to discover a lush nest composed of moss and soft grasses. Cradled gently in the back corner were seven eggs. They laid within a finely wound cup of some sort of fuzzy material. Each egg was about the size of my thumbnail,

Black-capped Chickadee eggs and a dime

beige with little brown spots.

How exciting! We were going to be the proud grandparents of a chickadee brood! I've always held a soft spot in my heart for black-capped chickadees and was most anxious to see what success they have in their nesting.

Our bluebird line at that time consisted of about 10 houses. Although we had yet to see bluebirds nest in them, we've had lots of fun year after year with the tree swallows that do use them.

One year we watched a male bluebird and a male tree swallow "duke it out" over possession of a nesting box. That year the tree swallow won, but he had to take the bluebird right down to the ground in their final battle for possession.

Our eventual goal is to attract bluebirds and every year we put up more boxes in different locations to increase our chances. Don't get me wrong, though, we dearly love the tree swallows - we're just hoping to attract both species to our yard!

The tree swallows are immense fun when they are building their nests. I had once read in *Peterson's Field Guide* that they like to play with white feathers. Off we trotted to buy some white feathers at the local arts and crafts store. We brought them home and took a few out of the bag. Then we would take a feather and toss it up into the air, letting the breeze catch it. It would float for a bit and then all of a sudden the swallows noticed it! The game was afoot!

One bird would grab the feather - usually just before it hit the ground - carry it higher and then let it go. Another would grab it up and swoop away into a different direction and let it go. Another would snatch it up and on and on the game would go until one of the tree swallows had had enough. It would grab the feather in a final decisive move and disappear with it into the nest box.

That in itself was an amazing feat, as the nest box hole is 1 1/2 inches wide and most of the feathers were 2 to 2 1/2 inches in length. Somehow the swallows never snagged one in the opening nor took it in the wrong direction. The angle of trajectory was calculated mid-flight and in they went in the blink of an eye.

When we opened the boxes a week or so later, further investigation revealed all of the white feathers to be woven into the swallows' grassy nests. When the fun and games were over, practical matters were taken care of by the swallows.

My brother-in-law, Don, was commenting that spring that he had seen quite a few swallows zooming around up and down the river near his home. Pat encouraged him to put up a nest box for them and gave him instructions. Don put up a nest box at noon and at 1:30 he called us to say that it was already occupied! Two tree swallows had already taken up residence in that short of a time!

My mother-in-law, Elsie, also told us that she was holding off from loading up her woodshed. It seems that she too was expecting a bird brood - but hers was a mother robin that had built a nest on top of her wood pile!

How wonderful our world can be and what a difference we can have in it. If you ever feel like you are insignificant and wonder why you have been placed on this earth, then put up a bird house. You will no longer feel insignificant, but will be overjoyed to see the birds use it for the very important purpose of raising their family. There's no better feeling than that!

Chapter Six

Serendipity

Our area up here in the Upper Peninsula is famous for its winter birds. We have just the right climate and the right feeding grounds for lots of "winter birds" that aren't seen in other areas. Many of the birds that come here in the fall and winter are able to find plenty to eat so they will stay here all winter.

A few examples are the pine grosbeaks, snowy owls, great gray owls, pine siskins, crossbills, and redpolls. These are all northern birds which will sometimes come south into the United States when they are in search of food.

The numerous amounts of berry-laden shrubs and crabapple trees keep many of the smaller birds hanging around, and the large, open hay fields keep the raptors coming back looking for more prey.

There are usually a few oddities that will also show up and it is these that the birders who come up here every year are looking for. Some of the harder to find birds include the great gray owls, the hawk owls, and the goshawks.

Pat and I have always had a good time talking with the bird-watchers who make trips up here from faraway places and we have opened our home many times for them to come in and watch our feeder birds from the comfort of our living room. Many a birder has left here with a "lifer" bird, whether it be a ruffed grouse, a pine grosbeak, or maybe a hoary redpoll.

Once in awhile, the birds that come in will even surprise Pat and I.

On a chilly winter day in February one year, a large group of birders had stopped in our driveway and it was obvious that they were looking for birds. Pat walked down the driveway and invited them all up to the house. They parked their cars down there and walked up to the house, looking for birds the whole time in the surrounding treetops and woods.

One fella asked Pat, "Say, what's that bird sitting up there in the tall tree just over top of your house?" Immediately about 12 pairs of binoculars focused on the rounded bird shape sitting alone at the top of a tall pine tree.

Someone said, "I can't believe it, but it looks like a goshawk!"

There were cries of glee and exclamations of wonder as the remaining birders also raised their glasses up to the sky. If it truly was a goshawk, that is a rarity and a bird that few birders have seen in the wild, as they are elusive and hard to find.

As they all looked at the bird, the identification was confirmed. That was indeed a fully mature goshawk. It sat there at the tippy-top of a 30-foot tall pine tree like it was in its glory. Its slate gray body was clearly visible and those people who had scopes quickly set them up to get a closer peek at it. They were able to see the blood-red eyes and the tiny hook on its beak - all in all a wonderful sighting. Everyone got a good look at the raptor before it finally decided that the place was getting too crowded and it took off into the woods.

The crowd then proceeded the rest of the way up the driveway and headed into the house for a much-needed break before heading back out into the cold day. You can bet, though, that that hawk was a highlight of the day for many of the birders!

The bull-bat

One lovely summer evening at dusk, we were sitting out on our deck casually watching the incredible flying acrobatics of our resident tree swallows.

Suddenly, I caught a glimpse of something larger out of the corner of my eye. Glancing north, I saw a large, long-winged bird swooping and diving over the edge of our hardwood forest. Then there were two, then three. Their flying antics were amazing as they darted to and fro, changing speeds and directions in a split-second.

As they neared the house, I observed the telltale patches of white on the wings that identified them as members of the nightjar family - the common nighthawk. I have always been intrigued by the tree swallows and their flight, but these birds were much faster and more fun to watch.

European folklore lists the nightjar family as "goatsuckers." This name was assigned because these birds were often seen flying over pastures and open fields in the late evening hours. It was assumed that they were slyly sucking milk from the farm animals every night. Although goatsuckers may not be their official name, nobody can contest that they differ from the rest of the birds in the family (which includes the common poorwill, whip-poor-will and the chuck-will's-widow) with their long-pointed wings, white wing patches, and slightly forked tails.

Other names that folks have used for the nighthawk have been port-and-beans, mosquito-hawk, burnt-land bird and bull-bat. Most of these nicknames stemmed from the sounds they make while flying.

"Beans" is one name for the nasally "peeent!" sound they frequently make while hunting insects. "Bull" is another name referring to the noise that bullfrogs make with their throats. The nighthawk makes a similar sound with the feathers on its wings during its mating flight.

To make the "bull" sound, the male hovers over and circles around the female, flying up high. Then he dramatically dives down and pulls up just before he is about to hit the ground. The air being forced through his primary wing feathers makes a noise similar to a sonic boom, although not as loud or as liable to break things.

After this display, the male then lands and begins to show off for the female by spreading out his tail, showing the white bar, and flashing tantalizing glimpses of his lovely white neck. Meanwhile, he calls and rocks back and forth to woo her.

Many years ago when I lived in Grand Rapids, I thought that a summer evening was not complete without the "peeents" of nighthawks flying overhead. Whether in the city or in the country, nighthawks are welcomed with open arms. Electric lights inevitably will draw bugs and the nighthawks, being the advantageous insectivores that they are, come in chomping with mouths wide open.

I could go to bed at night and rest assured that those pesky mosquitoes were being consumed in prodigious amounts. Indeed, as reported in the *Audubon Society's Eastern Region Field Guide*, researchers have analyzed the contents of a nighthawk's stomach and found that in one day a nighthawk ate over 500 mosquitoes. Another was found to have eaten 2,175 flying ants.

They even have bristles around their beak to help funnel the insects into their mouths. Some people call them "bearded" or "whiskered" beaks.

Nightly banquets by the nighthawks are made possible by their tiny beaks and enormous mouths. Most of them are nocturnal and they are known for their large, flat heads.

In actuality, the nighthawk was severely misnamed. They are neither hawks, nor are they entirely nocturnal. Its long, pointed wings, hawklike shape, and the ability to catch insects in the air caused someone to label it a hawk. Their main hunting hours are at dawn and at dusk, and even in broad daylight when they are feeding nestlings. They have excellent vision and hunt by sight alone.

Even though I enjoy the antics of nighthawks catching flying insects, I have never known anyone who has seen one on a nest. I can imagine that their gray/brown bodies sprinkled with black provide the perfect coloration for blending into the forest floor.

They choose not to build a nest, but instead will scrape out a slight depression in the dirt, rocks, logs, gravel, or on a rooftop to lay their usual two eggs. Nighthawks are known for disguising themselves in plain sight. Often they will perch motionless on a limb, usually lengthwise or diagonally on overhead wires.

When searching the skies for nighthawks, check the skies for a slim, darting, dancing form and listen carefully for the "beans" call from above. Be glad that those extra-large mouths of theirs are hard at work eating pesky insects.

Turkey herding

As I was leaving to go to work late one summer afternoon I had a strange experience. We live on a half-mile-long dirt road which is a dead end, so not much traffic goes down this road. Therefore, wildlife also feels that it is its playground. We have seen bitterns stalking across the road, herons standing gracefully at its edges in the ditches, and many geese and turkeys waddling along the sides of the road.

I turned out of the driveway in my truck and I could see some black objects in the road down farther. As I got closer, I could see that it was two turkey hens and a whole bunch of poults (chicks). The poults were long-legged and ungainly, but were big enough to have stubborn minds of their own.

One of the hens and two poults were on one side of the road and the other hen was on the other side of the road with about eight poults of her own.

The problem was that my truck would not fit down the middle of the road between them. I slowed down and tried to squeeze between the groups, hoping that they would veer off into the grass on the side of the road. All that did was make them start running. Now I don't know when the last time was that you saw a turkey run, but they are hilarious! Their legs splay out to each side and their whole body of feathers shift from left to right, almost like they are wearing a loose-fitting coat. Meanwhile, their head darts from side to side to look backwards because their eyes look off to the front and side normally.

So now I had 12 turkeys running down the road ahead of me. The hens were trying to herd the poults all over to one side of the road, but they kept changing their mind and switching sides right in front of me. There was no way I could get past them! Nor would they head off into the grass until they were all together.

Finally the right-side hen joined the one on the left and together they were clucking and gobbling to try to get the poults on their side of the road. Of course the poults were running all out and their legs were flying about kicking dirt and rocks every which way.

A few at a time they all made it over to the same side of the road. All this time I was driving very slowly behind them, not trying to stress or rush them - they were doing that to themselves!

When the last poult made it over to the left side of the road, then all of a sudden they vanished into the tall grass. Poof. They were gone. All I was able to see was the swishing of the grass as they passed by and the heads of the hens looking all over the place.

What a rush that was - turkey herding! If only I had had cowboy boots on, the scene would have been complete.

Wings of wonder

It was over two decades ago that I had occasion to visit the state of Florida. While there, I was able to observe one of the strangest birds that I had ever seen - the anhinga.

When I first saw it, all that was sticking out of the water was its head and neck.

It casually swam by our boat, as if birds were supposed to be swimming in rivers every day.

The anhinga strongly resembled a snake and it gave me the shudders to see it so comfortable in the water.

Anhingas are able to use their wings as well as their feet to navigate proficiently under water as well as above.

Later that same day, I saw the same bird, perched in a dead snag, with its wings spread open to dry in the afternoon sun.

The wings of birds can often give us definite clues about what they eat and how they live. Evolution has made sure that each bird species developed the exact type of wing that it needed to survive.

Wing styles vary from penguins which have shortened wings to help them "glide" through the water, to barn swallows which have dynamic, short, fighter-style wings that they use to quickly outmaneuver flying insects.

Other examples include:

• Hummingbirds have very short, stiff wings that flap at an extremely high rate of speed. This gives them the distinction of being the only bird species that can fly either forward or backward. The hummingbird can also fly a complete somersault and does not need to turn a certain way first before flying in that direction.

• Falcons, on the other hand, need the ability to fly swiftly and accurately. Therefore, they have narrow, swept-back wings that give them a high degree of control in executing high-speed dives and swoops to catch their prey unawares.

• Vultures are a good example of a large bird that can conserve energy with its wings. Their lifestyle dictates that they need long, broad wings to help them ride air thermals all day in their endless search for carrion.

• At the other end of the scale are the seagull and albatross. They have long, narrow wings that allow them to fly effortlessly for long distances over land or water. They also conserve energy by riding air thermals and updrafts over the oceans.

• A prime wing factor for many ground-dwelling birds, such as grouse, is the ability to fly fast to escape predators. They have developed short, powerful stubby wings to accomplish this goal. To them, a rapid escape is much more important than energy conservation.

• Waterfowl have their own needs as well. They need to get from one body of water to another as quickly as possible before a predator notices them. Therefore, they fly fast and in a straight line with their short, efficient wings.

• In observing woodpeckers around our yard, I've noticed that they have a method of their own for conserving energy. They look as if they are on a roller-coaster ride, as they alternately flap and glide on their way from one tree to another. They flap until they've gained altitude, then soar down towards the earth as gravity takes over, then they quickly start flapping again.

Looking at birds and how they use their wings can give us many clues as to which species they belong to. The shape of the wing, whether it be long or short, blunt, pointed, or swept-back gives us an instant marker on our way to positively identify a bird.

Sharing bird experiences

Readers of my column write often to share their own birding experiences - which I love! The only thing better than being there is to listen to someone else gleefully tell a story of their own...

Eagle Wonder

• Mary D. from Brimley wrote a lovely letter one day: *"You don't know me and I am not a 'birder', but I am definitely a 'bird-lover.' I never got around to telling you, until now, of a wonderful experience my husband and I had in the afternoon of New Year's Eve, 1999.*

As we sat in our family room looking out from our patio windows facing north on Whitefish Bay, we suddenly saw a big bird come swooping down and perching itself on a tall birch tree whose top had been cropped by the wind. The tree was situated at the top of our 30 ft. bluff among other birch trees about 75 ft. from the house. We had a perfect unobstructed view of this magnificent adult eagle.

Two of our grandsons (ages 11 and 15) were visiting us and were fortunate to witness this beautiful sight as well. The eagle sat there looking out at the lake for at least a full 5 minutes before taking off toward the water in an easterly direction.

Our dog (a lab mix) sensed something unusual, as well, for he stood silently staring at it for as long as we did.

We have seen eagles in our area several times a year since we moved here six years ago.

On another occasion I spotted an eagle perched on a ledge of ice that had piled up on the beach. As I approached the top of the bluff the adult eagle soared into the air and the wing expanse was enormous. He had some difficulty in his ascent, perhaps because he was so close to the water and very little surface for takeoff. However, in a matter of seconds he was gracefully airborne. Our grandchildren have seen them fly overhead and my husband and I have seen as many as 4 or 5 adult eagles accompanied by 3 or 4 immatures ones circling above the tall hill across the road from us.

We are seeing more pileated woodpeckers also. A few days ago as I stepped outside I saw two of these beauties chasing each other around a tree trunk about 4 feet off the ground and making quite a racket with their strange and unfamiliar utterances. As soon as they discovered my pres-

ence they flew across the road and darted around the nearest tree calling out in the same peculiar fashion. The fact that I intruded on them did not seem to concern them all that much. I just enjoy watching them.

We love the calls of the loons. Herons, geese, ducks and loons are our close neighbors. We will keep our eyes open for unusual sightings even if we are not 'real' 'birders.'

Birds and Water

• Al D. from Sault Ste. Marie tells us: *"I have to be careful. I do not want to get a severe case of the dreaded, time consuming, Bird Watcher Virus but I was checking out the Brimley Bay boat launch yesterday and there were 4 pairs of what I thought were Hooded Mergansers and another pair of Common Mergansers plus a large raft of one of the scaups. After checking my field guide I am not so certain on the mergansers. I have to go back this afternoon and see if they are still hanging around. Damn it, I may be already infected.*

I went out with my boat just to poke around in Munuscong Bay. On the first sand island you come to from the downbound cut are two trees only. There were 4 heron nests in one and 5 in the other. I saw two pairs of them. The bay is way down and it is going to be a difficult year for nesting ducks. Way too much exposed beach. The young will have to run a long gauntlet of seagulls that gulp newly hatched mallards down like they were marshmallows."

Warming up the birds

Even though we do our best to avoid it, there are still times when the birds hit the windows in our house.

It is always distressing, but we found that we have had good success in reviving and bringing the birds back from the brink of death.

Sometimes it is easy, and sometimes it is hard. No matter what, as soon as Pat or I hears that "whunk!!" sound against the window we scramble to see what hit it.

We are not always successful, but eight times out of ten we are able to rescue the hurt birds. Many times they are just stunned and all they need is a safe place to recover. We go outside and scoop them up into our hands and let them warm up. Unless it is obvious that they have broken their neck or their back, then we will pick them up. A bird that has broken its neck is usually dead right away. Otherwise, there is a good chance that they can survive. Shock is a huge factor and if we can warm the bird up and keep it from going into shock, they should be able to recover.

Keep in mind that we are not looking to keep a live bird, nor are we trying to capture it to keep it - both of which are illegal. All we are doing is helping them out a little bit.

Much of the danger of a window-hit bird lies in them laying on the ground. Raptors can scoop in and get them, as can cats, raccoons, and dogs. They are in an especially vulnerable position and subject to predation.

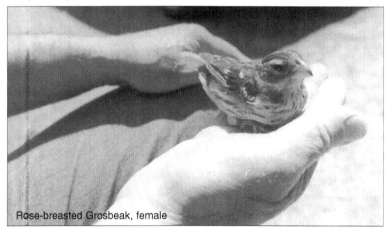
Rose-breasted Grosbeak, female

Over the years we have rescued pine siskins, goldfinches, chickadees, redpolls, grosbeaks, woodpeckers, nuthatches, and even a sharp-shinned hawk one time.

Usually, what we do is go outside and gently pick them up in our hands, then we hold them close to warm them up. I'll admit that we also talk softly to them, and even pet or smooth down their feathers.

Sometimes they'll have their mouths gaping open, or their eyes are shut or half-shut. As the birds recover, they will close their mouths and open their eyes all the way. Sometimes the recovery is real slow, other times it is fast. I would say it depends on how badly they stunned themselves or if they are hurt inside where we

Sharp-shinned Hawk

can't see it.

It is interesting that you can really see the personality of the species when you hold them in your hand. The feistiest birds are the siskins and the redpolls. They are so funny because they will try to really hurt your hands with their tiny beaks. Some of the bigger birds will surprise you because they really don't react too much - they just seem to sit in your hand and wait to see what you will do.

Recently a hairy woodpecker hit the windows at the back of our house. It hit so hard that it woke me out of a restless sleep.

Hairy Woodpecker, male

Pine Siskin

Sometimes we go outside and the bird has already flown away. With woodpeckers you never know - they have such hard skulls and are used to hitting hard on trees that you wouldn't think a window hit would bother them. Pat went outside to check out the woodpecker. It looked bad as it was jammed beak-first into the ground next to the foundation of our house. Pat picked it up and it was sitting still with its eyes half open. He held it firmly in one of his hands (he has large hands) and it didn't try to move at all. It

Rose-breasted Grosbeak, male

was working its eyes a little bit, keeping an eye on us.

I motioned through the window that I wanted to get a photograph. I went to get the camera and Pat moved it closer to the window for me. I took three photos and Pat loosened his hand just a little to give me a better shot. Then, all of a sudden, the hairy was struggling in his hand! I could see black and white feathers flailing everywhere. Pat opened his hand all the way and the hairy practically blasted up towards the sky. I guess it was tired of getting its picture taken!

Many times we will warm up a bird, then we will place it on one of the tray feeders in the sunshine to give it a few minutes to recover and get its bearings. Before we know it, the bird has vanished and our job is done. There's no better feeling in the world than knowing you have saved a wild critter.

Spring shagpokes

One spring a forceful rainstorm hit our area. On my way home from work there were signs of flooding everywhere I looked.

The field adjoining the yard of one of our neighbors was now a small lake and encroached upon the road.

Another neighbor was conducting a battle with a bulging stream which was threatening to wash away the base of his newly constructed driveway bridge. In every direction I turned, streams had turned into rivers and many yards were flooded from backed-up ditches.

When I was traveling down our dirt road, I observed the water blasting out of an eight-foot culvert, which is normally just a trickle.

I had just pulled into the driveway when Pat slyly said, "Want to see some shagpokes?" Need he ask? Of course I did. We walked across the road to our neighbor's property and watched helplessly while part of their driveway crumbled under the force of the rising beaver pond beyond.

Forming quickly on the other side of their drive was a new marshy area, probably temporary, but exciting nevertheless. We grabbed our binoculars and were using them to scour the marsh. I overlooked a short, dead snag ahead of me and was frantically searching when the snag moved! I had found what I came for, the elusive American bittern.

American Bittern

All spring I had been hearing the strange, watery, throaty sound that the bittern makes (OOnk-a-ChOOnk!) but was never able to pinpoint its location without the aid of hip boots or waders. Then, there were two of them, right in front of me.

They were a rich brown color with a distinctive, broad, black "whisker" running down their chin area. Their stout, streaked bodies and greenish legs were hidden in the lush deep weeds and grasses of this new marsh.

The American bittern is best known for its unusual camouflage abilities. It chooses not to flush when disturbed, but instead to "freeze" and "make like a reed blowing in the wind." The one I was watching would cock its head ever so slightly to see better and was immobile.

If I had not seen it move, I would have been easily tricked into believing that it was an integral part of the grass.

The highlights and shadows of the tall grasses and rushes in which it stood blended perfectly with the vertical streaks on its throat, head, and belly.

With its beak pointed skyward, it calmly gazed around at its surroundings. Every now and then it would break its pose, then hunker down and scoot to a new position.

Upon arriving at the new spot five or six feet away, it would then point up into the new "fake weed" position, all without a sound.

Occasionally, I've been lucky enough to hear the calls of the bittern. I have always thought that their call resembles someone pouring liquid out of a gallon jug too fast and it makes that "ga-glunk" sound when the air bubble comes out.

This strange sound has led many people to tag it with such nicknames as shagpoke, stake-driver, and thunder-pumper. Once heard, you don't forget the sound and it can be heard up to a half-mile away.

When bitterns are not frozen in position, they can be seen stalking their prey in slow motion. They will consume frogs, small eels, insects, and water snakes.

While I was watching the two bitterns in the marsh, I caught a glimpse of another large bird flying in. Incredibly, it was a third bittern coming in to take advantage of the temporary flooding and the unexpected food opportunities.

It was exciting to watch the change that came over the first two shagpokes when the new arrival landed. Instantly, they dropped down into the weeds and began a jerky, forced march toward the intruder.

It is possible that the first two were a pair, and that they were defending their territory, for they disappeared into a small wooded area shortly afterward and I never saw them again.

All in all, an awesome sighting of three elusive birds and their behavior.

I'll just go get it

One summer when Pat and I were at a craft show (as a vendor), we were approached by a woman whose hair was all awry and her clothes were all rumpled. She looked around at the bird feeders we were selling and she said, "Oh good, you know about birds." Then she sidled over to the side of our booth away from everyone else and leaned over like she wanted to tell us a secret.

"Can you help me figure out what bird I saw?", she said.

"What did it look like?", I asked.

"Well, it was brownish with streaks on its belly and it kind of had a yellowish wash to its sides," she replied.

"How big was it?"

"I think it was kind of like the same size as a robin, maybe."

"What kind of beak did it have?"

"It was a medium size, but pointy - I think."

"Where did you see it?"

"Oh, it hit my living room window, so I got a real good look at it, but I've never seen a bird like that before."

"When did you see this bird?"

"Mmm, maybe a month or two ago."

"This is kinda hard for us, I mean, without actually seeing the bird it is really hard to identify something that someone else has seen."

"Oh, well, that's OK. I'll just go home and get it for you. I've got it in my freezer!"

What? I thought. And then off she went, happy as a lark that someone wanted to see "her" bird. And I in turn was horrified that she still had it in her freezer. What? Was it tucked in alongside her frozen peas or laying next to its cousin the chicken breast?

That was a weird experience.

PeeWee the gull

One beautiful fall day many years ago, my mother-in-law, Elsie, noticed that her dog was worrying something in the back yard. The dog was playing with an object that she couldn't quite see so she went over to check it out.

It turned out to be a tiny ring-billed gull chick. Elsie picked it up and took it inside to help it recover. She had a tender heart for the little things and would raise anything that she got her hands on. The amazing part was how good she was at it. Elsie loved all critters, but she seemed to have a special fondness for birds and bunnies. Her son, Pat, has told me often that at one time she had more rabbits than could be counted - and that they all started with three little bunnies.

At this time, however, this gull received all of her attention. She hand-fed it scraps of food and basically domesticated it. Friends and neighbors all came over from time to time to see PeeWee. Pat recalls his Aunt Flossie making regular trips down to the house to visit PeeWee and she often brought friends down to see it.

PeeWee grew fast and he became quite spoiled. If you gave him your last sandwich morsel, he would pick it apart and discard the crust and only eat the meat.

Pat recalls one time when they were eating watermelon. They tossed a watermelon rind over to PeeWee and he gobbled that up faster than anything. The only problem was that he ate it so fast he didn't get it lined up right. For two days PeeWee walked around with a slightly curved lump in his throat (which it is said looked painful) where his crop would be. He looked ridiculous - like he had a distended and unusual Adam's apple. But he recovered nicely.

PeeWee was treated like a baby and he never had to open his wings or even try very hard to get food as everyone hand-fed him.

One day, after he had been there about a year, he heard and saw some gulls flying overhead. He opened his wings and flapped them a few times to see what they did, then he flew to the top of a nearby telephone pole. Once he had his eye on what was at the horizon, he opened his wings again and flew away - never once looking back.

From that day on, nobody came to see PeeWee again because he never came back. Occasionally in the spring of the year, a gull

Ring-billed Gull

would land on top of the same telephone pole (which they had never done before) and Elsie would swear that that was her PeeWee coming back to check on her.

Anne Trissell

It is not often that you meet a person who is truly compassionate and caring from the depths of their soul. I met such a person and her name is Anne Trissell. She lives with her husband Jerry and she used to live with many other companions, such as Earl Gray, Mr. Chips, Turkey Lurkey, Big Bird, and Poor Old Magee.

Big Bird is a regal sandhill crane who was brought to Anne 29 years ago when he was shot with a pellet gun. The pellets were not removable and his injured wing never healed correctly. He lived in a pen behind Anne's house and was friendly with her, but wary of strangers. When I approached too close, he retreated into his hiding bush. Anne told me that he likes to take pokes at their German Shepherd through the chain link fence as he runs by. Even though Big Bird cannot fly, that still does not prevent him from participating in the annual spring mating dance. When the migrating wild sandhill cranes fly overhead, he leaps, flaps and dances around, yet does not return their calls. He is not pressured for company, as he has a lovely hen turkey named Turkey Lurkey for a companion.

Turkey Lurkey has never been injured but comes and goes as she wishes. Occasionally, Anne has to retrieve her from the neighbor's yard, where there is a day care, as Turkey Lurkey likes to look at the children and scare them. In the early evenings, she flies out of the pen to catch a few bugs in the yard but returns later to bed down in the straw with Big Bird.

Turkey Lurkey is gorgeous with all her multi-hued feathers shining iridescent in the sunshine and she even allows me to stroke her back. Anne said, "She really likes it when you pet her head, she can feel it more." I have to admit that I am a bit apprehensive as a turkey's head is kind of weird-looking, being so wrinkly and all. Surprisingly, she puts up with me as I tentatively touch her head and run my fingertips over her bumpy skin. Turkey Lurkey closes her eyes in pleasure and I know that I've been accepted.

Anne accumulates strays from everywhere. Some stay only long enough to recuperate from their injuries and are released, others will stay with her a lifetime. Anne has gained a favorable reputation locally and has been called upon by everyone from her neighbors to the Department of Natural Resources.

One time the DNR called on her services to help them with a mute swan that was injured by some wires in the St. Ignace area. When the officer brought the swan to her, it was so large that it was all he could do to carry it. Anne was able to clean up its cuts and to give it a place to rest its injured leg. I was impressed by the size and beauty of this swan. He was almost recovered when I saw him and was to be released in a few days. It was a great opportunity for me to be able to see such a magnif-

Big Bird, a sandhill crane

icent bird up close and I was amazed that he allowed me to come near him.

Over the years Anne has helped and healed many kinds of birds and animals, from squirrels and groundhogs to ravens and eagles.

She had regularly taken in birds such as long-eared owls from Whitefish Point Bird Observatory who have strained their wings. They heal quickly under Anne's care and are soon set free.

Anne has a special permit to allow her to

keep and raise wild animals, but she is entirely self-taught. She reads and studies all she can on the care of wild animals. Most of her knowledge has come through trial and error and she tells me that no two animals are alike in their care. Sometimes they will even require different foods. That truth was evident as I watched her demonstrate her technique in feeding an abandoned baby pigeon. Normally the baby will reach into the parent's mouth to drink a "special milk" that the adult provides. Anne was able to mimic this by cutting off the narrow end of a nippled infant's bottle, allowing the baby pigeon to push its whole head in to feed, resulting in a messy process.

As Anne was cuddling the pigeon, behind us squawked another long-time resident, a yellow-headed Amazon parrot named Magee. He was yelling some sort of a jungle cry at the top of his lungs. He was captured in the wild as an adult bird and was not as trainable as a younger bird would have been, so he was given up for adoption. For 35 years he had traveled from one home to another until he found a home with Anne. He can holler as much as he wants out in the dog kennel and still receive his share of love when Anne comes in to attend the dogs.

The parrot was a sharp contrast to the recuperating raven out in the yard. He was utterly quiet and would retreat into a wooden pen whenever we came near. He too has a damaged wing and Anne was not sure if he would recover or not.

Anne was raised on a farm near Pontiac, Michigan, and it was there among the farm animals that she learned how to handle fowl and other wild animals. Her mother complained that she was forever bringing home dogs that weren't lost! She would bring a dog home that was sitting on the sidewalk, even if it was sitting in front of its own home!

Some of the animals that Anne had rescued were now her lifetime residents.

Mr. Chips was a beaver that was found on a roadside when its mother was killed three years before that. Anne and her husband raised him and now he romps happily in his pen complete with a water tub and a beaver house. After a few years, Jerry and Anne found Mr. Chips a new home with a wildlife refuge that was looking to stock its new beaver houses.

Earl Gray is another resident who zooms around his pen with glee. He is a silver fox that was probably released or escaped from a fur farm downstate.

All in all, Trissell is a valuable commodity in the Eastern Upper Peninsula. She is a vital member of the Humane Society and has taken care of animals when no one else will.

Her generous heart is evident in her deep love for all wildlife and she has saved the lives of more animals than can be counted.

Her husband, Jerry, jokes, "everything lives a long time around Anne."

Indeed, Anne is a rare gem in our world today because of her ability and willingness to make a difference where nobody else will.

Chapter Seven

Dusk magic with owls

One year, Pat and I were attending the Spring Fling at Whitefish Point Bird Observatory and we had decided to stay overnight so that we could attend the early morning bird walk the next day.

That afternoon we explored all along the Point, where the land juts out into Lake Superior forming a natural land bridge. It is here every spring that the migrating birds gather their strength before they head out across the big water to complete their journey. Over the years, we have always found this a delightful place to go bird-watching, as we never know what to expect.

We found all sorts of delightful birds there that day and a flock of ruby-crowned kinglets in a scrub pine was an unexpected find, as we had never even seen a single one before then.

We went to dinner and killed some time wandering around the town of Paradise, then headed back to the Point just before dusk. Whitefish Point is a wonderful place to look for all sorts of birds. Not only waterfowl and raptors, but also the smaller birds will cross there, if you are there at the right time and the right place. There is an elevated platform in the middle of the scrub pine forest where much of the migration can be viewed. It is here where you can see the raptors forming rafts (gatherings) overhead, waiting for just the right tailwind to help carry them across the lake. They will circle and circle, sometimes high, sometimes low, taking advantage of the warm thermal currents to carry them up and down on long wings. During the day, raptors like osprey, eagles, merlins, kestrels, sharp-shinned hawks, and Cooper's hawks would zoom over your head - sometimes what seemed like close enough to touch them.

During the evening, however, it was a magical time for owls. Owls had

Great Gray Owl

their own type of technique. They did not form rafts before they headed out over the big water. Instead, they were probably sitting in the trees around us all afternoon, taking naps and getting their rest before they attempted to fly across.

We went up to the platform and found it chock-full with bird-watchers, who were all waiting for the same thing that we were. We were all bundled up against the cold wind and there were lots of binoculars and scopes in sight, even though they were just about useless at dusk. Everybody's eyes were scanning the skies and the horizons, looking for the telltale shape of an owl. There had to have been at least 30 people standing on a 12' x 20' platform - it must have been amusing for the birds to see as they flew over-head. With that many pairs of eyes, no bird should have gone by unseen.

All of a sudden, a cry was heard, "There's one!" A lone arm pointed into the darkening air towards the south as a dark shape zipped towards us. There was murmuring and muttering while everyone tried to get their "knockers" up and focused. I just looked for the shape and then didn't look away from it. It was a large owl and it passed within 20 feet of the platform. Everyone spoke in hushed tones and the bird seemed oblivious as it was on its way towards an intense mission. The general consensus was that it was a barred owl, due to the shape, flight, and the coloring that could be seen.

Only a few minutes later, someone else spotted another owl, and then another one. Pretty soon we were turning our heads left and right and looking all around us as fast as we could. Sometimes the sight of the owl would be obscured by someone and it would seem like the owl would be right on top of you before you saw it! The owls had no compunction about clearing the platform with any great height and at times it seemed as if you could reach your arm up and touch them as they flew over our heads.

As it got quickly darker, it became harder and harder to spot the owls. There were large owls, small owls, and every size in between. Dark shapes zipping by at fast speeds and shadows bare-ly seen registered into our brains as distinctive owl species, usual-ly after the fact. "Hey, that was a great gray owl I think!" or "That was so tiny it had to have been a screech owl."

After it got almost completely dark, the only way we could see the owls was to look for their shapes against the barely still-lit horizon. Which meant that they were already past us when we finally saw them.

It was a magical start to our evening, and everyone on the platform that night was in awe of the sight of dozens of owls flying over their heads to places unknown farther north. It left a sense of wonder and mystery in our minds and we all walked away with a greater sense of the world unseen.

Landing in the snow

Sometimes bird-watching consists of nothing more than just making observations. That's OK, though, it's how we learn about birds.

One very cold winter day - I think it was below zero outside, I was watching the birds as they came in to the bird feeders in the backyard. It was very cold out, and I couldn't imagine that I would be moving around at all if I was a bird. I would be sitting someplace with my warm feathers surrounding me until the sun came out to warm me up, then I might go in to get some seed.

I watched the birds as they came in to grab some bird seed. The bird feeders were covered in snow, so many of the birds were attempting to land on the ground to look for seeds.

Each specie of bird seemed to have its own preference. The starlings abhor the snow and when they came in they would flap around and around until they could find a bare patch of ground to land on. Then they would lean out over onto the snow to pick at bits of whatever was on the top of the snow.

The mourning doves and the grosbeaks were different. They acted like they didn't care whether they landed in the snow or not. They came in with small groups of their friends and each one "poofed" down into the snow like it was just a whole lot of cotton. Then they marched around in the snow looking for seeds, just pushing it aside with their fluffy breasts.

The chickadees and the goldfinches didn't seem to care either. They just landed on the tray feeders and pushed their heads right into the snow in their search.

The grouse were funniest of all. They would fly in to the woods behind our house, then they would "swim" in to the backyard. What was funny was that you couldn't see their feet, they just zoomed around in the snow - it reminded me of the talking snowman that floated around in the snow in the old "Rudolph the Red-nosed Reindeer" movie. There was no obvious means of locomotion, they just magically floated from place to place.

Again, I may be a wimp, but I think I would have waited until the bird seed trays were devoid of snow, and then taken my time sorting for just the right morsel - keeping an eye out for predators the whole time, of course.

The trees were swaying

As I've mentioned previously, turkeys like to roost in the treetops at night. It was a nightly ritual for us to watch them get ready. Eleven or 12 turkeys would mill around in the woods beside our house for 15 minutes or so when it was getting to be dusk. They would absentmindedly pick up things on the floor of the woods and drop them, delaying the inevitable, I think.

Then they would slowly migrate to the front yard, stopping to look at bits of whatever in the grass. Now and then one of them would glance up towards the trees, almost like they were picking out their spot ahead of time.

Next, one of them would make the decision to go. It would stop

Wild Turkeys

what it was doing, look at a particular tree for a second or two, then run as fast as it could across the lawn for about five or six steps, flapping furiously the whole time. Halfway across the lawn it would lift off and then fly straight up - right into the trees.

Now mind you, turkeys are not graceful at all. When they land on a branch, it's more of a crash landing with a scramble of wings and feet to grab the branch before they fall back down again. Even if you were blind, you could hear the turkeys as they crashed into the tree and the skittering of scaly toes on tree branches.

After one got going, then all of the rest of the turkeys would take turns running across the lawn, sometimes even forming a line with each choosing their own tree for their roost. Branches would be flying and breaking as they attacked their chosen spot. Sometimes, they would change their mind and flap like crazy to make it to a different branch. Or maybe they would be sagging down too much from their weight that they would sidle along to get closer to the tree trunk.

Turkeys don't really fit into the silhouette of a tree. Most of the branches and leaves hang out in a diagonal fashion, with a few going up and out. And then here are the turkeys, a straight verti-cal blob with two skinny stick legs. They don't exactly blend in! But the key to the whole adventure is that the turkeys are safe from predators in the trees. They can close their eyes to sleep and not have to worry about being attacked.

One day when they were all up in the aspens, Pat and I noticed

Wild Turkey

that the wind was blowing strongly. We also noticed that the turkeys were already up in the trees so we pulled up chairs and settled down to watch the show.

It didn't take us long to figure out that the turkeys weren't having too much fun. They were swaying from side to side and were bouncing up and down on the branches like mini trampolines. They were gripping the branches with their long toes like they were hanging on for dear life - which they were!

Every now and then a branch would break from the stress and the turkey would go tumbling down. It would open its wings and frantically scramble to grab another branch before it fell all the way down to the ground.

It was a bit like watching the circus - you didn't know who was going to entertain you the most, so you had to watch all the performers at once. Each turkey had its own method for dealing with the wind. Some stood tall and tried to go along with the movement of the branch, like doing the "wave" at a baseball game. Others squatted down and tried to present the least amount of resistance to the wind. It was fun - and almost painful - to watch.

However, it wasn't long before it got too dark for us to watch the turkeys anymore. We were able to get a short videotape of them while they were swaying and swinging - that should be good for some entertainment someday!

Who would've thought that turkeys can dance in the treetops?

The red, white, and blue of freedom

We Americans choose to live in our freedom, often taking it for granted and not realizing how lucky and fortunate we are. Birds also live in their freedom, without knowing that they do so. An eagle soars high above us in the sky with the greatest of ease, flaunting its own personal freedom and its lack of physical ties to the ground. It is free to pursue its prey in the air or to court a mate by cartwheeling around him/her in the same air in which it hunts.

All birds exhibit what, to us, must be the ultimate freedom. Why else would the glorious bald eagle have been chosen as the symbol of our nation - other than that it stands proud and regal, sure of itself in its power and with the freedom to live its own life.

Most Americans have someone in their family who at one time or another has fought to keep our country free. Perhaps they are veterans, in which case the red, white, and blue have a special significance.

As the American flag with its patriotic colors snaps to attention all over the country at certain times of the year, we as a people should take the opportunity to experience and enjoy our freedom. One way to do this is by using our sight. The brilliant red of one of our most native birds, the Northern cardinal, mimics the red stripes of our own flag.

Many other birds are also willing to share our patriotism by displaying their own portion of bright red - like the head on a Red-headed woodpecker, the crest on a pileated woodpecker, the breast of the rose-breasted grosbeak, the cap of the common redpoll, or the entire body of the scarlet tanager.

Not to be outdone, many other birds participate by displaying the most brilliant blue that they can grow.

Examples include the shocking blue of the blue grosbeak, the incredibly iridescent blue of the indigo bunting, or the softer blues on the bodies of mountain bluebirds, eastern bluebirds, blue jays, or lazuli buntings.

Our birding flag just wouldn't be complete without the purity of the white stripes to finish it off. This white is evident on the bellies of the red-eyed vireo, the Eastern bluebird, the slate-colored junco, the downy and hairy woodpeckers, and the barn and tree swallow.

Other birds getting into the act would be black-capped chickadees with their white cheeks and the breast of the white-breasted nuthatch. For the ultimate showing, though, we have to congratulate the mute swan, the snowy owl, the whooping crane, and the snowy egret.

If one were so inclined to place together a cardinal, a blue grosbeak, and a snowy owl, we would have the most brilliant flag of all, It would be an outstanding living display of the three colors, that when thrust together, should evoke a strong sense of patriotism in each of us.

Just as we know to stand and place our hands over our hearts

during the playing of the national anthem, so should we cherish
our freedom each day as the birds do - by enjoying each moment
as it comes and living each day to the fullest.

America,
Home of the brave and
Land of the free,
Together myself and my
Avian friends salute thee.

Horned grebe episode

Al D. from Brimley recalled an incident that happened at the
school where he worked, *"One of the gals in my classroom found a*
stranded and helpless horned grebe in the middle of a county highway in
early April. She brought it to me in a makeshift cage with corn in the bot-
tom and it was a miserable little specimen. The ponds and rivers were still
frozen and this little guy came north too soon.

It must have become exhausted flying around looking for a body of
water to land in. From a duck's eye view, the black asphalt of the highway
must have looked like a river. Normally, I do not take in these creatures
as it does not take long for you to get a reputation as a wild animal reha-
bilitator and bingo. Everyone is bringing you their injured and orphaned
wild things. I greatly admire the people that dedicate their lives and basi-
cally all their spare time to these animal saving endeavors but I never
allowed myself to become entrapped.

But upon peering into the box and seeing this small grebe sitting in
corn kernels and lettuce, I relented just this once and took him home. I
realized that it would no doubt come to an end not fitting for an uncom-
mon grebe if I did not take him.

I put him outside in an open cage with a large stock pan full of water.
It promptly slid in and drank the water. That was a good indication that
I had a chance of saving him.

So I started a force feeding program with small pieces of smelt and as
his trust and hunger grew, he became a voracious little eater. But the nice
thing now was that I only had to offer him his smelt tidbits from my fin-
gers. He promptly gobbled them down.

I do not recall how long I had him but the ponds became ice free and it was time to release him. One morning I took him down to an extensive swamp-like body of water. A very nice release site as there would be plenty of minnows and other things for a grebe to feed on. And plenty of take off space should he decide to go elsewhere.

When I slid him into the water he just exploded in joyful dives and wing beatings and he swam around in circles and much to my surprise ... came back every now and then for another piece of smelt.

After I loaded him up on enough smelt to take him through his rehabilitation time I walked to my van and drove away. I had a bit of a hard time leaving him but he belonged in his wild environment."

Observations

Observing the birds is a year-round hobby. It doesn't matter if it is winter, spring, summer, or fall, there are always some sort of birds around somewhere. Spring and fall, however, are always my favorite times, as there are more chances to see migrants and unusual birds that one doesn't normally get to see.

No Fear

• From Rudy W. in Barbeau: *"The fishing is so poor here in Barbeau that we have a handicapped seagull, bad right foot, coming to our feeder and eating apple peelings that we put out for the birds, squirrels and deer. Also cracked peanuts.*

Also it appears that mother osprey has her nest about ready on #17 channel marker. It is a pair and for the last several years a nest has been built on the marker in the river. About two years ago a platform was built for them to use and they use it. The nest appears to be about three and a-half-feet in diameter and almost 2-foot thick.

It is unbelievable how large some of the sticks are. I know a pair has hatched at least one and fledged one for the last three-four years that I have been watching their efforts.

These birds are getting used to the water traffic as you can pass within 30-40 feet of the marker and not have them fly."

Bird Breakfast

• Also from Allen D.: *"I used to fish Munuscong Bay a lot many years ago and there was a large number of nesting herons (50 or so) off a point called Maple Point at the south end of the bay. Because of very low water conditions I did not go that far this trip but I see no reason why they are not still nesting there. The small bunch I saw last week are no more than 10 minutes boat trip from the place I saw the turkeys. I do not know what species they are but they are indeed herons.*

A friend of mine who many years ago had a couple of nesting semi-domesticated mallards hatch their broods in his backyard pond and he related to me what he witnessed helplessly. A flock of seagulls came out of nowhere and as he said, 'gulped the newly hatched ducklings down like they were marshmallows.' I would not be a good nature photographer as I would have had to interfere with their feast.

And oh yes, I forgot to tell you that a pair of osprey were in the nest above the channel marker light right off the Church Camp that is being sold to the DNR. Also the cormorants were out in force."

New Bird

• Julie T. from Brimley sent the following nice note: *"We have had a male yellow-headed blackbird at our feeders for the past two days. We have seen him for two days now. He is beautiful and really stands out with the flock of redwing blackbirds he is with. At this time at noon he is inside one of our feeders. We have seen these beautiful birds in our travels west in WI, MI and ND and this is the first time we have seen them this far east.*

Also this morning we were graced by a great blue that flew over the house on the way to the beaver pond out back."

Hummer in Hand

• Violette W. from Pickford called to tell me about a neat experience she had. *"I found a female hummingbird that was flying around inside our pole barn. She was going around and around practically beating herself to death trying to get out the windows. I waited and watched until she got tired, then picked her up and held her in my hands. She was so soft, like a delicate silk, and she was very warm. She quieted right down when I held her in my hands. I took her outside the barn and set her on a branch. It wasn't long before she flew away!"*

The nesting king of the skies

First, I glance all around me. I see nothing. Then I look up at the wires above me in the air. Still I see nothing. The coast seems to be clear as I cautiously approach the fence post. Fifteen feet, then ten, then five feet away. Just as I am about to lean over to peek into the nest on top of the post, I hear an explosive chatter behind me and Pat says, "Look out!" I duck down just in time as an Eastern kingbird zooms down to buzz me across the top of the head. I can hear her wings fluttering as she flies past me and I see her begin her return.

As is their nature, Eastern kingbirds will attack any animal or bird that comes into their territory, no matter what the size. It doesn't matter if the intruder is just flying by overhead, posing no threat to the nest, or simply walking by. The kingbird will immediately take up pursuit to drive the interloper away. Sometimes they will strike in the back and sometimes they will purposely try to pull feathers or hair out to get their message across. Kingbirds have been seen forcing squirrels into deep cover and they also have been known to knock bluejays (who are known egg eaters) right off their perches.

Truly the kingbird must live up to its name and reign as "king" over its entire territory, whether that space be vertical or horizontal. Any animal or bird (or human) entering that area is subject to attack. Research studies have proven that this aggressive defense ensures a successful brood will be raised. The Eastern kingbird enjoys one of the highest nesting rates due to this aggressiveness.

Indeed, on that very day, the mother kingbird would not let me anywhere near her nest, even though I only wanted to take a look. She also will not tolerate cowbird eggs in her nest. Even if a cowbird were to somehow get through her defenses, she will simply roll the offending egg out.

The *Audubon Society Field Guide* comments that the Eastern kingbird sometimes chooses unusual locations to build their nests. Over the past three years, we have watched them build in our yard in three very strange places:

• Year One: They chose an artificial flowering azalea to build in, constructing the nest in and among the sisal/styrofoam base. It actually was quite a lovely creation, with an assortment of grasses and blue and pink yarn added to it. I tried to persuade her into

Eastern Kingbird chick

using some red yarn as well by placing it on the edge of the basket, but she wouldn't have any part of it, tossing it off arrogantly into the wind. Nesting Success: three eggs laid - three babies fledged.

• Year Two: They chose the top of an old fence post to build on, with an assortment of grasses and long, white yarn from an old mop we had laying about. It was interesting to note that this seemed to be a very hot location, as it was in direct sun all day. Mother kingbird (or father) would spread her wings to form a sort of "umbrella" for the baby during the hottest part of the day. Nesting success: three eggs laid - one baby fledged.

Eastern Kingbird chicks

• Year Three: This year they chose the most unusual location of all. The nest was in an empty flower pot nailed to the top of a fence post on the edge of our neighbor's driveway. For some reason the pair were extremely defensive at that location. I snuck a peak and found four eggs that had hatched but I couldn't seem to get close enough for photos (the surrounding ground is tough to walk in). Nesting success: four eggs laid, four babies fledged.

Once their babies hatched, both mom and dad faithfully guarded the nest. They were constantly on the lookout for intruders. Some of their favorite perches are power lines, fences, and empty branches, where they issue challenges to all would-be enemies. Their harsh, repeating "killy - killy - killy - killy" calls and loud twitters are intimidating when they rush you by flying right at your face!

Years ago, when the lone baby hatched out of the fence post top, I had an occasion to watch mom (or dad?) stuff an entire dragonfly down the hatch of the waiting fledgling. That was not an easy matter for either participant, as the dragonfly was just as wide as it was long.

Whenever we would venture near any one of the kingbird nests in any year, the adults would dive-bomb us every time. As I drove by with my truck, it was cute to watch four fuzzy blind heads instantly pop up out of the pot. As if on cue, when one of the parents let out a twitter, all four beaks snapped open.

All this is viewed from a distance, however, as the kingbird is not quite what you would call approachable!

Little looky-loos

I will make no bones about it - birds are snoopy. As humans we are a bit vain (ya think!?) and we put windows in our houses so that we can see outside. And yet when something tries to look in at US, we get all bent out of shape.

Humans are not the only ones that are "peeping toms" - birds are too! Our bird feeders in our backyard are only about eight feet from the windows in the back of our house. Is it possible that the birds are trying to get even? That they are tired of being stared at (by us) all the time, and are going to give us a taste of our own medicine?

When the hummingbirds come up to the window nectar feeders to feed, I never get the impression that they are looking in the window - they seem to be too busy getting a drink. However, when a male purple finch perches precariously on a tiny lip of a window and peeks in at us I start to wonder.

We've had birds of all sorts look in the windows. When the turkeys started doing it, I began to be suspicious. They would come in first thing in the morning and walk around the backyard. If there was no birdseed in the feeders or on the ground for them to eat, they would wander up to the windows and make it a point to look in at us. What can be going through their naked little heads? Are they trying to give us hints that the birdseed is gone?

Purple Finch, male

Are they giving us a visual reminder that "we are here now - come out and feed us!"? If so, they are not very subtle.

One time a yellow-bellied sapsucker perched on a bedroom

Yellow-bellied sapsucker

window and sat there for about 10 minutes. It didn't make any noise, nor did it move around a lot. There were plenty of flower stalks, tree branches, and other objects around for the sapsucker to land on, why would it pick the difficult place of a slippery window sill that is only about a quarter-inch wide?

Woodpeckers are also "peeping toms," as are chickadees and pine siskins. They have all perched on our sills from time to time and looked in at us.

What do they see? What must they think? Can they even see anything inside the house? Are they judging my housekeeping skills? For goodness sake, I sure hope not.

A glimpse of green

As I sat at my desk doing a little work, a glimpse of green caught my eye. I looked out the window - there was nothing there. I went back to my work when suddenly I saw another flash of green. When I glanced through the window again - I saw them - zoom! zoom! Two ruby-throated hummingbirds flew past me like bullets at what seemed like 100 mph. Twenty minutes later, they were still battling one another, protecting some unseen territorial bounds around the hummingbird feeder outside my window.

Anyone who is familiar with ruby-throated hummingbirds knows what fascinating little birds they are. Indeed, many people landscape their gardens and yards to specifically attract hummingbirds.

Ruby-throated hummingbirds are the only hummers that are regularly found east of the Mississippi River and are the only ones that are known to breed in the Eastern United States. They are Michigan's smallest bird and they weigh less than a penny.

The hummingbird is named for the unusual sounds that its wings make in flight. These same wings will beat up to 80 times per second and allow the hummer to fly like no other bird on earth. Hummingbird wings are short and stiff and can be rotated in virtually any direction. They are the only bird that can fly backwards, fly a complete somersault, and can also hover in one spot for an indefinite length of time. This hovering ability is what allows them to feed on tubular flowers. They hover below or in front of the flower tube and insert their bill into it - while using their long tongue to lick out the nectar. I recently watched a beautiful male do this to just about every blossom of my bleeding heart plant. That was no easy task as it has over twenty individual flowers on each stalk.

Many people have the misguided notion that hummingbirds "suck" nectar, but they do not. Instead they lick it out with their long tongues and I have seen them flickering their tongues afterwards, sort of like they are "licking their chops."

Even though nectar is a favorite food, they cannot survive on liquid alone. Hummers also eat ants, aphids, mosquitoes, beetles, gnats, and spiders. They especially like spiders, for more than one reason. They will eat the spider, plus whatever juicy insect happens to be hanging in the web, then possibly take a little of the silk webbing to bind their nest together.

It is the female who does all of the nest work and the raising of the brood. She is not afraid to defend her nest, even against large intruders like humans. A hummingbird nest is a delicate and carefully camouflaged affair and can take awhile to build.

She will construct her two-inch (!) nest out of plant material and hold it together with lichens to conceal its location, usually in the branch of a tree in a forest clearing 10 to 20 feet high. Finally, she will lay two pea-size white eggs. Because of their small size, and the fact that they are so well hidden, very few hummingbird nests are ever found.

I had the opportunity to observe the hummingbird's interesting mating display one day. A female hummer flew past my nose while I was sitting on the deck, then sat quietly in a pine tree beside me. Next, a brilliant male zoomed in, his red throat shining iridescent in the sunlight.

He located the female sitting demurely within the tree, then proceeded to fly in a "U" shape in front of her, buzzing all the while. Back and forth he dipped and rose, again and again until even I was impressed with his flying prowess.

Eventually the female flew up to join him, directly confronting him and off they flew into the sunset together.

Both the male and female can be identified by the metallic green color on their backs and underneath they are whitish-gray. Their tail is fan-like with white tips and they have a needle-like bill. The male has a bright red throat called a gorget. In the sunlight the hummer backs shine just like an expensive jewel and the individual feathers on the male's throat glisten like glitter.

I have seen photos that people have sent into various magazines, where they have 10 to 25 hummers at one feeding station. That may happen when the hummers are in migration and not defending territories like they do in Michigan. At our house the hummingbird, whether male or female, is very territorial. Very rarely will even two of them sit together at a feeder and when they do, they are very wary of one another.

I have often watched a single hummingbird "guard" the feeder on and off all day, either sitting on top of the hanging hook, or on top of a nearby swing. From there he would chase away anyone who tries to get a sip. Sometimes when he was off chasing someone away, a third hummer would sneak in for a quick drink while he wasn't looking.

Hummers have the highest metabolism of any warm-blooded vertebrate and they must eat constantly all day long. To do this they are in constant motion, only stopping long enough to rest when checking for interlopers or when nest-sitting. They will also go into a trance-like torpor at night to lower their body temperature and conserve energy.

All in all they are fascinating little creatures and one that I never get tired of watching.

A living room surprise

We used to rent a small house that sat out in the middle of an open field on top of a hill. There was a spot of woods only fifty feet away on one side. It was in these woods that we would occasionally see owls sitting when it got close to dark. Usually a barred owl, but sometimes great horned owls would also grace us with their presence. We had our bird feeders situated in our front yard on the woods side so it was only natural that owls might gather close by. During the day in the wintertime, sleek deer mice, fat voles, and moles would be seen coming up out of holes in the snow to snatch a few seed morsels before disappearing back into their holes again. Who knows what went on at night?

One day I was walking through the living room on my way to do who-knows-what when I saw a glimpse of something out of my left eye. I looked through the windows and I jumped back a bit in shock. Wow!! There was an owl sitting on the top of our snow gauge - which just so happens to have a bird feeder attached to it. And not only that - it was the holy grail of owls - the great gray!

I don't know if you know anything about great grays, but they are our tallest owl in North America and they are impressive, especially when seen up close. Oh my, I knew this was a special moment. I said a short prayer to keep the owl there while I slowly backed up and headed into the bedroom behind me to grab my camera.

I slowly snuck back out with my camera all ready to go. I was hoping that the owl was distracted enough by his hunting that he wouldn't notice me getting in position in the house. It was busy out there and its head was spinning from left to right and from top to bottom looking for some of those birdseed-fattened little rodents. I was indeed able to take a few photographs and was torn between watching the owl with fascination and taking photographs to preserve the moment. I knew nobody would believe me if I didn't get photos!

Luckily, it gave me enough time to see it that I was able to do both. I was in awe of its size and beauty and wished the moment could have lasted longer, but I'm sure it was only a minute or two.

Because there was nothing showing itself under the bird feeder, it was time for the owl to move on.

One last glimpse as it flew away revealed incredible feathered legs and feet, which you couldn't see when it was sitting on the gauge.

That's the normal bird thing - being in the right place at the right time!

Great Gray Owl

Chapter Eight

Empty nest syndrome

The beginning of August is always a sad and lonely time around our house. Many of the frenzied summer activities that our birds are involved in are now slowing down.

All of the tree swallows have raised their broods and left their homes. It was only a few short weeks ago that their many chattering cries filled the air above our home every evening.

Each of our 13 bluebird houses hatched out an average of two tree swallow babies. Many nights there would be over two dozen brilliant blue-green-backed swallows darting everywhere catching and eating bugs by the gross.

We would like to think that's why we aren't plagued by too many mosquitoes this year. Now, though, the swallows have moved on to airspace elsewhere, teaching the youngsters how to fly and showing them the surrounding territory for future returns.

The Eastern kingbirds have already raised their babies and are even now teaching them how to hunt insects on the wing. Now that the fledgling's wing and tail feathers have fully developed, the parents have set to the task of teaching them the fine details of flight. Pat was able to watch the last nestling fledge. The baby teetered on the edge of the flowerpot nest for a few minutes, with the mother twittering from a nearby branch. Finally off he flew, and the mother kingbird took wing to join him, flying directly underneath him, supporting and guiding him to a nearby bush.

For a few weeks, the parent kingbirds were hanging around with their whole clan. The nestlings were so cute, as they were lined up all in a row on the barbed-wire fence. One by one, the mother or father would feed them, whether it be a juicy worm or a still-wriggling dragonfly. Occasionally we would see the odd kingbird, in passing, but the trees around our house were quiet and missing their lively chatter.

Pat also mentioned that he saw a great blue heron pair fly above the field near our house. They were flirting and courting with each other the whole way. It was over the same field each day that he has also been observing an American bittern fly back and forth, over and over again. We think that she is hunting and bringing back food for her little ones, which is always an exhausting task.

August is also the goldfinches' time of the summer. The bull thistle plants have released their down and the finches are busy primping and finalizing their nests. Each year, they patiently wait for the thistle to bloom so that they can have exactly the type of soft nest they desire. As I watched in wonder, a bright yellow male dipped through the air above the house, over and over again, warbling his song of enticement to any female goldfinch who would listen.

Sadly, no longer were the parents bringing their fledglings in to the bird feeders. We were lucky enough to watch yellow-bellied sapsuckers, purple finches, evening grosbeaks, chickadees, woodpeckers, and nuthatches all lead their newly fledged babies to our feeders. It was on our myriad selection of feeders that they learned how to scratch for fresh seed, cling to vertical and slanted surfaces, and how to properly enter and exit feeder openings. Here it was also that they learned how to keep one eye on the skies overhead for danger and where to zip into when the alert cry was given.

I would also like to believe that it was at our house that many birds got their first taste of sunflower seeds, corn, and peanut butter. And that they will remember us when they return from migration in the following years.

Fishing for chickadees

Pat tells me this story about a day that he was deer hunting. Many years ago he was sitting out in his deer blind on a beautiful fall day. He hadn't seen any deer all morning and was bored. He had seen a few squirrels and heard and seen a few birds, but nothing yet with antlers.

Pat grabbed up his sandwich and was eating it when a chickadee popped out of nowhere. It landed on the ground in front of him and was searching for the bread crumbs that Pat was leaving. Over and over again the chickadee would drop down to get some crumbs, then fly up to a nearby branch. "Hmmm," Pat thought, "I wonder if it'll eat any more?" So he broke off a tiny piece of his sandwich and dropped it. The bouncy little chickadee jumped all over it and swallowed the morsel right up.

Pat then got the strange notion to see if he could catch the chickadee - he was bored after all. He pulled on a nearby tree and broke off a little branch. Then he looked around his blind and found a piece of an old tow rope. He twisted it apart and took just one strand off of it, then tied the strand to his little branch to make a miniature fishing pole. Fishing and hunting was Pat's forte' and he was really curious to see if this would work.

Pat fashioned a loop out of the end of the strand and then laid it on the ground in front of him with the stick in his hand and a sandwich piece inside the loop.

Amazingly enough, when the chickadee came in to grab the bread, Pat pulled the loop tight around one of its legs. It worked! The chickadee tried to fly away, but was tethered to the string which Pat was holding onto. "It was wild - that little bird was flying around and around on the end of the string!" Pat said. It was kind of like a living balloon and the bird was frantic to get away. He brought the line down and pulled the chickadee into his lap, where he then grabbed lightly ahold of it to calm it down. He held it firmly in his hand while he took off the string from around its leg.

Pat was always thinking of what he could do to stir up mischief at deer camp, so he then stood up and walked a ways over to where his brother-in-law Chuck was sitting in his blind. Pat held out his hand and Chuck said, "What have you got there?" Pat then opened his hand and the chickadee exploded out of his hand and into Chuck's face. Chuck violently recoiled, and fell off of his chair, cursing all the way!

Pat laughed and kept a smile on his face the rest of the afternoon. As for Chuck, Pat said he never forgave him for that little stunt!

Birding world vs. man's world

I have sometimes wondered how the birding world would be different if it wasn't for the wonderful inventions of man.

Birds would definitely have fewer perches if it weren't for the

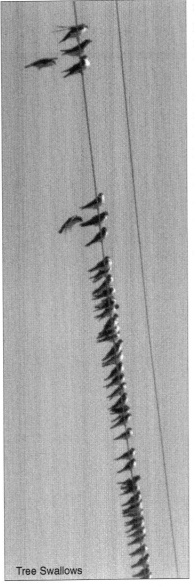

Tree Swallows

multitude of utility wires, fence posts, barbed wire fences, and rooftops that man has managed to erect over the decades.

There is a belted king-fisher that I have observed many times on M-129 near Tone Road. His main perch is the telephone/power line that strad-dles the creek there. From his vantage point along this unnatural vine, he can easily scan the water for fish and simply drop-dive into the creek. A tree branch is not as convenient nor as sturdy.

Along many of our back roads are lots of prime hunting areas for hawks. The kestrels sit upon the continuous string of manmade wire to peer over the fields and ditches for any errant or unwary mice. These lines provide the "ultimate" viewing areas, being unobstructed by branches or leaves. The same power lines in the fall are also the gathering grounds of many flocks of European starlings. They will group together by the hundreds near freshly mowed hay fields. A passing car will send the whole flock into the air, and just as quickly, they are back onto the lines again, jostling for position.

Eastern kingbirds also use the overhead lines for hunting perches. Up there they can scan their whole kingdom and easily leap off the wire to snatch bugs out of the air.

Cliff swallows and tree swallows favor utility wires as well. Long-winged birds such as these do not like to sit too close to one another, as they could become entangled when landing and taking off. They instinctively know to leave just about a "wing's reach" between them for personal space. Often many hundreds of cliff or tree swallows can be seen late in the summer as they feed in large groups and prepare for the migration flight ahead.

Although convenient, utility lines are not always the safe haven they appear to be.

One fall day a neighbor called us to report an unusual spectacle on 23 Mile Road. Birds too can be caught in freak accidents. We drove to the site and witnessed something that I have never seen in my entire life. Hanging upside down from a power line were three dead Eastern kingbirds. Many people driving in the area assumed that they were bats. But they weren't. Speculation has it that the line was either struck by lightning or that the wind snapped the two lines together to complete a deadly electrical connection.

The birds did not have enough time to leap off the line before they were electrocuted. Due to the fact that they were sitting on the line when it happened, their little feet were still locked onto the wire. Their lifeless bodies still dangled helplessly with their feet clutching their last perch. Although it seems morbid, death too has a part in the daily struggles of the avian world.

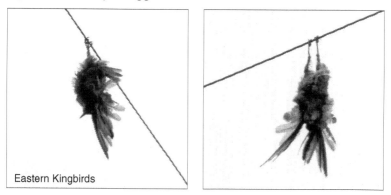
Eastern Kingbirds

Another commonly used manmade item is the good old fence post. A long time ago when Pat and I were traveling through Alberta, Canada, we saw over a dozen red-tail and rough-tailed hawks perched on fence posts along the road. With miles of corn fields surrounding them, I guess the fence posts were the only perch within sight!

From the tops of these posts, each hawk jealously guarded their own little territory and screamed their anger at any human (such as us) that dared to stop and videotape them. A mini-drama unfolded before us one day as we watched two red-tail hawks fight over a mouse that one had caught. A brash young hawk tried to knock the resident hawk with the mouse off of its perch so that he could snatch the juicy morsel. Instead, the mouse owner chose to fly off with his meal clutched in one taloned foot, surrendering his fence post to the intruder.

I can't count the number of times I have seen ravens and crows on top of fence posts as well, usually all ruffled up. I imagine them debating in their minds where to fly that particular day in their search for food. Where would they sit to make that major decision if not on a post. How kind it was that some farmer put those out there just for them.

Observations

A Neat Experience

• From Marv D. in Brimley: *"My wife and I just had the neatest experience. About 7 pm this evening we were en route to some property we own north of Rudyard from our house in Brimley.*

We spotted a Great Gray Owl sitting on a fence post about a quarter-mile south of Lockhart on Bound Road. We stopped and turned around and watched it for about 10 minutes. Another car stopped and a lady got out and walked all around it and took pictures.

We went to our property and worked for about an hour. We returned about 8:05 and it was still there. We then returned to our house, picked up the camera and returned about 8:30 and I took about 8 pictures which will be questionable due to the dying light.

It finally flew into some conifers on the west side of the road when I tried to get closer than the edge of the road. But there was no doubt about it being a great gray. What a sight!"

Feeder Competition

• Jarl H. from Sugar Island sent this quick note: *"This summer morning, almost midday, I saw something amusing at my hummingbird feeder. A female came to the feeder with some whitish object in its bill, dunked it thru one of the portholes and immediately took off. They've learned 'dunkin' donuts!' Soon, as usual, the male came by to supervise, however a yellow jacket wasp discovered him on the perch and quickly chased him away. It is interesting to note that two male hummingbirds will feed together (without combat) but did see two females 'duke-it-out' at the feeder. There also seems to be less patronage now that the lilacs are in full bloom."*

A Dedicated Bander

• I met a man named Dr. Ludwig in September of 2000. He was a dedicated bird bander and had been so since 1927. At the time that I talked to him, he had been banding birds down at his house on the St. Marys River. He said, *"I've been banding gulls and terns for 74 years now. I started off doing it in Lansing High School and have been doing it ever since. I've traveled all over the world and have seen 247 different species of birds from here to Midway Island/Hawaii. Over the years myself and my sons and grandsons have banded up to 12 birds at a time totaling over 630,000 birds banded."* He also mentioned that his son lived nearby and that he has been banding gulls for over 20 years.

Migratory Sightings

• I received a wonderful note from Leroy P. in September of 2000 that was a delight to read: *"Autumn is in the air - and on the water too. Many common EUP birds can be seen gathering for their journey south. Our family was sailing Lake Huron toward Cheboygan. About two miles south of the Les Cheneaux Islands in the direction of Bois Blanc Island, we noticed what looked to be a large new island where one had never been before. Now, we all know that Great Lakes waters haven't receded that much, yet!!*

With binoculars we could see that this apparent island was undulating and in motion. As the black mass approached, it became clear that it was a massive flock of cormorants winging toward us just above the water's surface. There was a moment of concern about this flock overwhelming us (i.e.: Hitchcock's 'The Birds').

That feeling quickly fell away as the birds quietly separated and left a wide buffer around our boat. We were amazed by the vast number of these large sea birds. We have noticed a gathering of hundreds of cormorants many times. This flock our son Phil guestimated to be 10,000 birds. I thought 3,000 - 4,000 was more realistic. Certainly the largest crowd of birds, of any type, we have ever encountered.

One week later, Labor Day weekend, we had a similar encounter on Lake Huron with a notable gathering of loons. About 50 - 60 of these large majestic-looking birds were swimming and diving for fish about 5 miles southwest of the DeTour lighthouse.

We were thrilled as we had never seen more than a handful of loons together in one spot before this. The birds seemed unconcerned as we sailed among them. Our experience with loons finds they quickly dive when we venture too close. Finally, it brought to mind that we have never seen a Loon in flight. Are they just too uncommon of a bird, more water-bound than flying, or do they simply fly at night (those red eyes)?!!?

Our last unusual encounter with a large group of birds was on the way to the Chippewa County Fair, Labor Day morning. From a distance we could see a group of soaring birds. Soon we identified about 40 Turkey Vultures circling above the fields along M-129.

We regularly see gatherings of ducks and geese at spring and fall as they migrate through our area (or take up residence on lush lawns and golf courses). We surmise that these cormorants, loons, and turkey vultures are also gathering to take part in this enormous bird migration."

Wrong place at wrong time

Every spring we try to make it up to Whitefish Point Bird Observatory to watch the birds. Inevitably we almost always see something there at that time of the year that we have never seen before.

WPBO is situated on a peninsula that juts out into Lake Superior, making it the perfect staging point for birds who are migrating north or south. By following the shoreline they can find the place to fly across "Gitchegoomee" at the shortest point possible, therefore staving off exhaustion and hunger. In the spring (and the fall!) the birds will often hang around in the trees and the dunes around the beach waiting for the perfect tailwind to help them fly across the vast expanse of water.

If a bird watcher is diligent enough, and determined enough, he or she can find birds hiding in the pine trees and the bushes around the Point. There are also many birds that are ready to fly across and they just plain take off and head along a beeline straight to the other side. They are usually oblivious to what is below them or around them and can be directly observed as they fly overhead.

All in all, WPBO is a magical place, filled with the wonder of unexpected encounters and the mystery of the unknown and the hidden.

One beautiful spring day Pat and I arrived at WPBO and we parked in the parking lot. Reports from the Point had been promising and lots of raptors and even flocks of small birds were already flying through the Point area. We got our gear together - you know, mittens, binoculars, Kleenex, and the like (it was still cold outside) and we headed towards the hawk platform to get some good overall views of the surrounding dunes and scrub pine forest.

Pat said he had to get rid of some coffee first, so we headed towards the public restrooms as our first order of the day. I stood outside the building, looking around and seeing what other people were looking at while I was waiting for him.

All of a sudden, I caught a movement out of the corner of my eye. I glanced up and was struck with awe as I saw the belly of a gorgeous adult osprey fly right over my head! I swiveled around to follow it with my eyes as it quickly flew past me and right on through the air towards the lakeshore. It already had eyes only for the other side and was powerfully pumping its long wings to get a great headstart.

I stood there with my mouth hanging open and I was thunderstruck for a few moments. I had seen a few ospreys from afar - quite often through binoculars, but never that close! It had to have been only ten feet over my head as it flew by. It just skimmed over the top of the buildings and kept right on going.

Needless to say, 30 seconds later Pat came out of the bathroom and wondered what was wrong with me. I was standing with two or three other people and we were all sharing our sighting of the osprey by excitedly sharing the details of it all over again.

I've said it once and I'll say it again, timing is everything with bird watching.

Canada Geese

Bird's egocentricity - especially about streets

Even birds, like people, can tend to be a bit egocentric at times.

Geese, ducks, and turkeys, for example, assume that the roadways were built just for them to walk on. Waddling across a flat roadway certainly must be easier than parting grasses and weeds to get to your destination. I'm sure that everyone has run into these self-assured birds at one time or another.

Just a short while ago, Pat and I were traveling downstate when I saw a flock of wild turkeys headed up out of the roadside ditch. They - the three hens and about two dozen half-grown chicks - were making a beeline straight for the road. Sensing their purpose, I started to slow the truck down. Without so much as a sideways glance to check for oncoming "anything," they proceeded to march single file across the roadway. They were not in any rush, of course, as they didn't have any appointments except a dinner date with the lush green grass on the other side. As they were getting closer to the other side, I nudged forward slowly and three or four of the young jumped violently. It must have been that they didn't trust our truck because they tried both leaping and flying, at the same time because their wing feathers were not fully developed yet.

A few minutes later, they had completed their crossing and I proceeded on my way. Maybe a less compassionate person would have continued driving through the flock, with feathers flying left and right, but the thought of an extremely large game bird in the radiator was not very appealing.

Another such incident occurred last week when we were driving down Portage Avenue in Sault Ste. Marie on our way home.

As Pat approached the Sugar Island ferry dock across from the Sault Ste. Marie Public Golf Course, a group of two adult Canada geese and about eight goose teenagers came up to the road's edge. The previous wild turkey crossing had given us "wild bird confidence" so we thought we would try it again.

Believe it or not, one of the adult geese looked both ways, then began to lead the way across the blacktop. When they were almost over there, the stragglers at the end were severely lagging behind the others. I thought that they needed a little incentive to hurry up.

A little toot on the horn from us fired them up and they began to rush toward the truck, honking wildly all the way. They set upon attacking the front tires until they were satisfied, then they rushed across the road to catch up with the others. That was not quite the reaction we had hoped for. We had to wait until the goose siege on our poor little truck was over before we could proceed. If a goose could give us a nasty look, they did. I guess geese can't be rushed!

Other birds that have crossed our paths recently when driving have been sandhill cranes. Early in the morning they often can be seen strolling with their long, long legs from one side of our road to the other. Do the long grasses tickle their undersides as they walk? Maybe the running is better on one side of the road than the other. Perhaps the small stones feel good on their toes as they step across the rough gravel road.

If that is the case, I'm sure we can expect to see more of them. In the meantime, I suppose I should put a bumper sticker on our truck reading, "We brake for birds."

Northern Flicker

More nesting joy

Another of our joys has been watching a pair of very interesting common flickers raise two handsome fellows (gals?) in a tree near our garage. They ignored the fine houses Pat built for them and instead excavated a new hole about 12 feet up in a nearby snag.

The parents made frequent trips to our ant-laden yard for snacks and made loud protesting noises whenever we accidentally got too close. It was a strange and wonderful sight when finally the two fuzzy heads popped in and out of the tree opening, always hungry and demanding of course. Then one day they were gone as well, almost like they were never there at all.

One of our resident purple finch pairs was so successful in bringing up their baby that it literally outgrew them. One day the three of them appeared on a tray bird feeder and we were able to watch the dedicated parents desperately feeding their now-grown cowbird.

The robins around our yard were not quite as lucky this year. Their nests always seem to be awkward creations, crafted of mud and grasses, usually in a precarious, tipsy spot. The nest that Mrs. Robin built in the pine tree in our yard was robbed of its eggs by hungry common grackles. I never get over the fact that some birds

American Robin nests

prey on other birds' eggs. Anyway, between the grackles and the blackbirds raiding the nests, only one of our three robins' nests raised a brood. Instead of robin fledglings, our yard was littered with empty sky-blue egg shells and broken nests.

Whatever happened to the black-capped chickadee pair that nested in one of our bluebird boxes remains a mystery. They laid seven eggs originally and one night three eggs went missing. Then the next night one more disappeared. There was no sign of the nest

Black-capped Chickadee eggs

being disturbed in any way but all of the chickadees had vanished, including the adults. Snakes maybe? Raccoons? Three eggs were left behind and they never hatched (obviously). We're not sure what happened, but we weren't chickadee grandparents that year.

Just move a feather

No matter how often I watch birds, I never tire of watching them fly. There must be a bit of jealousy there, as it must be a wonderful feeling to move your arms and be weightless in the air.

Birds are acrobats in the air, some more than others, and the ability that they take for granted is one that man has sought for hundreds of years. The Wright Brothers proved to us that learning to fly is a long and dangerous process and the story of Icarus showed us that it could be deadly.

One can't help but be jealous when watching a long-winged bird like a vulture or an eagle soaring through the air. They seem effortless as they float lazily through the air currents and the movement of just one tiny feather can alter their height or direction.

In watching birds, I have often noticed how they really do enjoy flying. It does not seem like just a way to get from one place to another, but instead can be a true joy to them as well too. All you have to do is watch crows or ravens in the springtime as they merrily cavort in the air. They will do somersaults, flips, quick turns, and halts in midair. There is no doubt in my mind that it is fun for them, like a high-altitude game of tag where you don't dare touch one another.

Gulls are another bird that enjoy flying. They are often seen soaring through the air especially on windy days where they can show off their expertise. They zoom from one place to another, then twist a crucial feather and change their direction in a heartbeat. They ride the breezes like a cowboy riding a bucking bronco and always come out ahead. It is amazing sometime how they can almost appear to be motionless in the air when there is a strong wind, with their head moving from side to side to check out the ground below them. Then, again, they move a tiny feather at the end of their wing and they gently brush off the wind, lower their landing gear and down to the earth they come.

How fun that must be.

A deadly turkey dance

One beautiful summer day I was sitting in the house relaxing when I heard the most bizarre sound. It sounded like something was screaming, then clucking, then there was a high-pitched keening sound. I could not figure out what the heck I was hearing! I did know, however, that it wasn't in the house. I walked out onto the back porch and I could hear the most awful racket in the woods behind our house. I could also see some movement in the clearing through the trees, so I headed back there, walking as quietly and as cautiously as I could. When I got closer to the sounds, I could see turkeys and they were all dancing around in the clearing. I knew this was going to be something neat, and they didn't notice me so I went back to the house, got the video camera and grabbed Pat too.

He and I headed back there and the turkeys were still at it. It was a large flock of about a dozen turkeys. There were a few hens and they were standing in the "wings," watching what was happening but not participating in any way. They too ignored us as they concentrated on the action. The turkeys in the center of the clearing were all toms and jakes of different ages. Four of them were locked in a heated battle. The jakes were dancing around the edges while the larger toms were paired off and circling one another. Every one of the male turkeys seemed to be making a different type of noise. Some were clucking, some were crooning and the combatants were almost screaming at one another.

Every few seconds the toms would rush towards one another and they would use their beaks to peck at the head of the other. It seemed as if they were aiming for each other's eyes, which to me was extremely grisly and disgusting. This was not a dance at all, it seemed as if it was a mortal battle!

Beaks were flashing, feet were flying and every now and then one of the tom's would catch a piece of the other one and they would be locked together for a few minutes. They would bite each other's heads and necks - wherever and whatever they could grab ahold. Sometimes they would pinch the wattles or every now and then they would be holding each other beak to beak. Then they would stare into each other's eyes and continue to trot in circles while holding each other. It appeared to be a deadly dance, one which we were able to watch in amazement. They really could have cared less if we were there or not. Every now and then they would walk around one another and then some silent signal was passed and they would open their wings, flap up a tiny bit, then bring up their feet with the spurs aimed towards the other turkey. No blood was seen, but the sight of those long spurs being used in battle was a bit frightening, at least to this human.

It was a vicious thing to watch but it really got the hens all stirred up - which I suppose was the purpose of the fighting. The hens most of the time were pretending not to watch, but they never strayed too far away and every now and then one of them could be seen glancing towards the fray. Flock dominance and the right to "have a go" at the hens was at stake there that day. Not wanting to disturb the "scene," we grabbed a few minutes of video, then retreated back down the trail. That was a sight not many people get to see - and we were both horrified and awed by the bloodthirstiness of the turkey!

More about hummers

Pat was involved in a heated discussion with a woman who lived downstate who insisted that hummingbirds do not have feet. She emphatically used her finger to point out that they never land on anything and that hummingbird feeders don't have perches because they can't land without feet.

Say what? This is ridiculous nonsense. How could anyone believe that? All birds have feet. All birds also have wings - they may be small and ineffectual, but they are still wings.

In fact, as I was writing this, a hummingbird dangled his little legs below him as he checked out a petunia. I could SEE his legs - so yes, they definitely have feet.

I was able to hold a hummingbird in my hand a few months ago, and yes, they do have the cutest little pixie feet imaginable.

Even though, at 3 and a-half inches, they are our smallest bird, hummingbirds have amazing endurance. For their size, they are an extremely strong flier and are able to travel long distances to reach their wintering grounds, which are in central Mexico and Costa Rica. They are even able to complete the long flight across the Gulf of Mexico. And no, the old wives' tale that they hop on the backs of geese for a ride is not true!

Hummingbirds continue each day to delight and amaze me. When our lawn sprinkler is running, I can see a male zipping in and out of the arc of the water, chattering all the while. Pat has also had them visit him in the garage when he leaves the big door open - of course, they are just checking out the red ball that he has hanging from the garage door. Inside the garage, hummingbirds' wings sound like a helicopter, and as quick as one, off they fly into the day.

In other words, to summarize, YES, all birds have feet, even hummingbirds. Remember that old round-bodied legless toy called a Weeble? And the jingle that went with it, "Weebles wobble but they don't fall down." Remember, a hummingbird is NOT a weeble.

Chapter Nine

The brave chicken

Pat and I have always been an adventurous couple, at least a decade or so ago when we were younger. We are starting to slow down now and the trips are often fewer as it takes us longer to recover afterwards!

However, when we were on our honeymoon 16 years ago, we decided that Alaska was where we wanted to drive, as both of us had always wanted to go there. To make a long story short, I'll tell you about an unusual town that we passed through while we were driving on the highway in Alaska.

We were tooling along in our truck when we passed a sign for the next town which was called "Chicken." We giggled about that for about five minutes and wondered why in the world the towns-folk would ever name a town after such a common bird.

Out of curiousity, we turned off the highway and went into Chicken, which was just a little blink of a town. Pat pulled into a party store parking lot and we went inside to get a few snacks. Then we wandered across the street to get a bite to eat.

We inquired with a few of the locals to find out how the town got its name. According to the rumors at the diner, the town's fore-fathers wanted to give their town a grand label and chose to name it after the official state bird chosen by Alaska's schoolchildren, the Willow Ptarmigan.

After much heated discussion amongst them on how to prop-erly spell "ptarmigan," they gave up and named the town after the common nickname for the state bird - Chicken.

This same bird was irregularly seen in Michigan many decades ago and even then it was uncommon. The last reported sighting of a willow ptarmigan was in 1920. Attempts to introduce the ptarmi-gan into Michigan's Upper Peninsula in the 1950s were unsuc-cessful.

However, when driving though Alaska, the ptarmigans are a common sight if you watch carefully along the side of the road and in the low scrub bushes which line the road. Willow ptarmigan are known to be a fierce defender of their nests, even chasing off humans and grizzlies.

Robert H. Armstrong, author of *Alaska's Birds*, tells of watching a male ptarmigan pounce upon the back of a Northern harrier to drive it off. All in all, a brave bird to have a town named after - well, sort of.

Bird bills

Evolution has, for many more years than Homo Sapiens have been around, been shaping the destiny and appearance of birds. As a result, birds are uniquely suited to their environment and have developed many interesting variations and specialties to survive in each of their habitats.

Birds have adapted to live in almost every known habitat in the world from frozen wastelands to lush green rain forests.

Their body shapes, feet, wings, bills, and eyes have all been shaped by time and experience to allow them to explore and survive in their own particular niches in the wilderness and/or cities. Birds' bills, in particular, are most fascinating to me because of the amazing variety in size, shape, and function.

Look at a pelican, for instance, and compare it with a chickadee. Everything about them is different and each would starve if placed in the other's habitat and expected to survive on similar foods.

By observing the bills of birds, we can determine their food sources and usually their methods of food retrieval as well.

For example:

- Ospreys, eagles, and owls have hooked bills that are the perfect tools for tearing and ripping the flesh of small mammals and birds.

- Herons and egrets have long, pointed bills which are the perfect "spearing" weapons for fishing, especially when coupled with a long, spring-like neck and lightning reflexes.

- Creepers have bills which curve downward, allowing them to probe deep into cracks and under the bark of trees for burrowing insects.

- Woodpeckers have short, stout bases with "whiskers" at the base, allowing them to hammer away at trees, either removing bark or excavating cavities in which they can detect deeply buried insects.

The whiskers keep the fine flying sawdust out of their eyes and mouth. Woodpeckers' bills are slightly chisel-shaped and they also utilize their long tongues (which wrap around inside their skull) with tiny barbs on them to withdraw insects.

- Chickadees, titmice, and wrens have very tiny bills for plucking insects from their hidey holes and for eating tiny seeds.

- The finch family, in general, has a conical bill for both cracking open and shelling seeds.

- Goldfinches and pine siskins are also able to probe deep into thistle heads to extract seeds with their tiny bills.

- Grosbeaks and cardinals have conical bills as well, but they are much larger and stouter than most of the finch family. They are even able to split open cherry pits and pull out large chunks of food.

White-winged Crossbill

- The crossbill is an extremely specialized finch. It has a special bill which can extract seeds from pine cones and it can also pry bark off of trees to expose sun-shy insects.

- The pelican also has an unusual bill, which is superbly suited for diving for fish. Including the pouch underneath, the bill can hold almost three gallons of water, hopefully, with a fish in it as well.

After exploring these many avenues of different bill types, I have also come to realize that with every birding example, there are exceptions.

Many birds, such as jays, starlings, and gulls, have what we could call a "general purpose" bill. Their particular bills do not reflect any specific food choice, but instead allow them to feed on a variety of foods. Any new food source provides them with new dining opportunities and they will immediately take advantage of it (ever notice how bluejays seem to appear out of nowhere when your bird feeder is filled?).

A bird in the hand...

A business owner named Jim told Pat this story recently when they were "talking birds." Jim said that there had been a big party out at his Dad's cabin one night. Of course, he had been there for the good time and he was also there the next morning. Many of the party guests were still sleeping off their big heads but Jim was up early wandering around the property cleaning up the mess. As he was picking up things he noticed that some kind of a sparrow was following him. Everywhere he went the sparrow trailed along behind him. Jim kept looking at it, trying to figure out what it was doing.

Then, just as a whim, he put out his hand and held it out in the sparrow's direction. To his utter surprise, the sparrow jumped up on his hand! Not only that, but the sparrow stayed put when he moved his hand around. Jim moved his hand to his face and looked at it, then tried walking around with his hand held out and the sparrow sitting on it. The sparrow stayed on his hand!

This was just too weird. Jim still couldn't believe it, and he knew that nobody else would believe it either when he told them later, so he decided to show somebody.

Jim walked up to the cabin, then opened the door - still the sparrow stayed on his hand. He went inside and used his other hand to wake somebody up and show them that this wild bird was sitting on his hand! And he wasn't holding it there either!

Of course, you can imagine the response he got from someone sleeping off a party time. Jim still remembers it to this day, and still bemoans the fact that not everybody believes him.

Observations

A Rare Sighting
- From Lt. J.S. Gray: *"I was recently in Brimley hunting with my*

brother-in-law. When I returned home my sister had wrapped smoked fish in your paper for the return trip. I happened to read your article on Ivory-billed woodpeckers. I was very shocked to find out that they are rare. I have not been to Ft. Campbell since 1994 but in a hunting area in the Region of the (LBL) Land Between the Lakes near the Kentucky/Tennessee line close to Dover, Tenn. on the Cumberland River. I have seen at least two pair of nesters. Without a doubt these are your birds.

Secondly, I live in southwestern lower Michigan and my hunting partner Gary S. has seen this type of bird in Alamena Township Swamp. He called it a Shunk Crow."

Make sure you wear your boots

• Merrie N. from Sault Ste. Marie was telling me about her bird experiences: *"I had been using a deer mix and sprinkling it around by the spruce trees for the grouse. Every day I had a ruffed grouse that liked to follow me when I walked down my trail. It would stay about 2-3 feet away from me, but still follow me all the way. My neighbor Charlie says that every time he mows the lawn that he has a grouse chasing his lawn mower. It must be 'protecting its territory.' Also, my husband Randy has taken to wearing boots when he uses the push lawn mower in our own yard as the grouse bites the back of his ankles when he mows!"*

Loons

• Allen D. from Sault Ste. Marie sent along this observation: *"There are lots of loons up where I go fishing in Canada in the Ontario game preserve. I observed a loon beating its wings enough to raise up as it rapidly pummeled its feet just on the surface of the water creating a splashy great commotion and then would settle down and put its head under the surface. Then I began to make a connection with the young bird(s) being under water and some distance from the parents. I am hypothesizing that this is a form of communication to the young that stray underwater. I am betting the young loons respond to this as a location device. On the surface they are always calling their young. I love listening to their cries in the late eves and early mornings. I will check back with you on what you think when I get back, unless the black flies suck out all my blood."*

Dusty birds

It is a fact of nature that birds have bugs on them. They can be infected with lice, mites, fleas, and all sorts of nasty, tiny bugs. While this may bother some people, it bothers the birds even more.

Signs of an infestation may include scratching with the feet or digging into the feathers with the bill. Another thing that birds do to relieve the symptoms of things biting them is to "dust" themselves. For some reason, birds have found out that a good layer of dirt on their skin eases their itching and gives them some relief, at least temporarily. However, birds don't like to get their feathers dirty, as then their feathers aren't as effective as usual. So what do they do? They dust and then they preen. This leaves a layer of dust/dirt on the skin, but gets the feathers clean.

Turkeys are well known for dusting and they will use practically any bare patch of ground that they can find. If the driveway is being used too much, they will notice that ugly bare patch of ground in your yard where you can't get any grass to grow and they will make it larger and deeper for you - wah! Or they will look to see where the rocks are the fewest in the driveway and then stir up the sand and dirt by plopping down and using their wings as a sort of "scoop" to brush the dirt over their heads, bodies, and tails. This is a violent-looking action, as it looks like they are fighting with something when they do it. They will stir up the dirt for awhile, then they will stand up and give a mighty shake of the whole body. Of course, on a turkey - whose skin and body feathers seem only loosely attached - this means that their whole

Ruffed Grouse

dusty, feathery contraption moves from side to side and it looks like everything is going to fall off. Then off they go to wander to find a safe place to preen for awhile.

Mourning doves have also been seen in the various piles of dirt around the yard. They are interesting because they are the same color as the dirt and it can be hard to see them when they are dusting. You may look outside and see a puff of dust rising from a bare patch of yard or in the driveway - that would be a dove.

Or it is possible that it could be a ruffed grouse dusting. The grouse don't always pick the most convenient places, at least as far as I am concerned. I will sometimes catch them dusting in my flower beds in the spring before the first buds start to come up. Another favorite place for the grouse is a standing pile of topsoil that we have in our back yard. The adults choose the base of the pile to do their dusting in and it's actually an acceptable place as far as I am concerned, as they can't hurt anything there. There have also been times when I have seen the adults bring in the young so that they can dust in the pile too. The chicks like to run up and down the pile of dirt and then spread themselves out anywhere from the bottom to the top to do their dusting.

All I can say is that it must feel good!

Beautiful appointments

Every few months when writing my newspaper column, I find I have to stop and regroup to organize my thoughts. Every now and then I have to clarify my writing objectives and refocus. It would be easy to wander into the quagmire of game-bird hunting politics or to descend into the murky depths of bird terminology and bird classification. Rather than tackling issues which are out of my control, I instead choose a lighter view, one of continuing to share my observations and bird-lore learning not just TO you, but WITH you.

I hope to convey the sense of wonder that I continually feel when birding in our area. That feeling was renewed recently when I passed through the Rudyard area. There, alongside highway I-75, was over a mile of sandhill cranes, gathered together in small family flocks, eating, flapping, and generally conversing with one another.

I imagined their conversations to be something like, "Should I leave tonight or tomorrow?" Or, "Do you like the grasshoppers or the spiders best here?" Or perhaps, "How many days do you think the journey will take us?"

Just the sight of so many of these ungainly, prehistoric-looking birds was enough to take my breath away. How many there were! And how lucky I was to see them. That moment will never happen again in that same way, even if I were to journey there a second or third time.

All too often, our lives fly by in a hurry and we fail to grasp the fleeting moments of beauty that unfold before our eyes each day.

Think not how annoying that hollering robin is at 6 a.m., but instead be glad that you have the hearing to appreciate his song as he gladly heralds each new day. Revel in his joy as he sings with all his soul. Listen with your heart, not your ears and let the robin be your guide.

These quick birding glances are yours alone to experience. A few days ago Pat and I were zooming down 15 Mile Road in Barbeau when he caught a glimpse of blue. Not only did we see a bluebird on the utility line, but there were also four more dashing around in a nearby bush.

How can I describe the bright blue of a bluebird's back to someone who has no sight? I could compare it with the blue of the sky or the blue of the summer weed called Chicory, but that's assuming that they have seen those things.

We can choose to walk around with blinders on, seeing only what we choose or we can open ourselves to each new delight unfolding in front of us.

Each season in Michigan brings new sights. Even though our swallows, sparrows, kingbirds, wrens, and sapsuckers have already migrated, there is still an abundance of activity everywhere.

If you travel down just about any country road in the area, flocks of different kinds of birds are gathering and preparing for their long journey south. Starlings, blackbirds, geese, cranes, and hummingbirds are eating like crazy to build up their energy reserves.

Meanwhile, goldfinches are molting into their fall coloring and the chickadees are searching for good winter roosting spots to last them through the upcoming cold winter nights.

One of our Barbeau neighbors, Moe, told us that Cloverland Electric gave him the reason for the minor power outages around the area as "all the birds on the utility lines." Indeed, many power lines are heavily laden with birds. The amounts are staggering.

I observed a flock of birds in Lake City a week or so ago that flew over M-55 and I thought that it would block out the sun, it was that huge.

We roughly estimated that the flock contained 10 to 20 thousand birds and smaller flocks of 300 to 400 were constantly breaking off and rejoining the main group.

As the birds (we think they were a mixture of starlings, grackles and blackbirds) flew around us, it was almost like a living creature, flowing and stretching through the sky. I have often wondered why they never crash into or bump one another.

It astounds me how quick their reflexes must be - whereas we humans cannot walk through a crowded mall hallway without bumping and jostling one another.

We also observed a large "V" formation of Canada geese already on their migratory journey. They were up in the sky at least a half-mile, maybe more, and I quit counting at over 300 geese on one "V."

There are wonders all around us. The robin sings not merely to annoy us into wakefulness, but to stick to his own agenda of being "the early bird which gets the worm."

A sad and lonely world this would be without the mournful honking of geese flying overhead or the wonderful musical whistles of the goldfinches flocking in for thistle seed each evening.

We need to slow down and enjoy the beauty rather than rushing all the time.

Teach yourself to live a life which is full of beautiful appointments with nature each day.

Kingbird with a crown

The Eastern kingbird is quite a bully of a bird, but I'm telling you, they are the ultimate parents as well. I have seen kingbirds do things to protect their broods that I have never seen other birds do.

One spring I had a fake, hanging, flowering azalea plant in our front yard hanging on a shepherd hook, along with a nesting-material bin and some other bird feeders. It seemed like we had a kingbird (or was it two?) that was constantly being seen in our front yard. Every time I looked outside I could see it hunting from the clothesline, or perhaps flying back and forth from the house to the woods. Finally, we were able to put two and two together and we noticed that the kingbirds were constantly going to the azalea plant and disappearing into it. They must be building a nest!

We waited until we could see one of the adults flying out of the plant, and then we zipped outside to take a look. Gently, very gently, we pulled the fake leaves back to see what was in the interior of the pot. Oooops! There, staring back at us was a pair of beady black eyes! We carefully replaced the leaves to keep her hidden on her nest and left her alone, but not before discovering that she had made a lovely nest out of brown grasses and pink and white yarn. It looked very soft and inviting and she wasn't moving from it! That was when we discovered that kingbirds will readily accept and use short pieces of yarn in their nests.

Eastern Kingbird

We tried laying pieces of white yarn on the edge of the plant basket and they would always disappear into the nest, to be weaved in with care and love.

However, when I laid a few pieces of red yarn on the edge of the basket, the adults would start hollering and get all bent out of shape until they were able to toss that out of the basket with their beaks.

For some bizarre reason, white and very light colors were their favorites. From then on, we always made a point to make sure that we left pieces of white yarn out in the grass of the lawn in the springtime so that the kingers would have nesting materials.

Eastern Kingbird

That white yarn was popular with the kingbirds. One fine, early spring day Pat noticed one of the kingbirds coming back and forth to the grass and grabbing up pieces of yarn. The bird seemed always to be in a bit of a hurry and was trying to grab up as many pieces of yarn as it could get in its beak at once. It didn't want to make any more trips than it had to. A few times Pat wasn't sure if

Eastern Kingbird

the kingbird would be able to fly because it had so much yarn in its beak. Then, somehow it would still be able to see over the bunch of yarn and off it would go. He laughed when he recalled how one time it came down and it kept getting the yarn all tangled up when it would try to grab more. For a second or two, the kingbird was comical because it looked like it was wearing a white turban! The yarn was all tangled up around its head and was gathered in its beak. A second later the kingbird took off to deposit its load in the nest. Turban or not, the job was getting done!

Here's a bittern at you

One day while Pat was working in his garage workshop I went down to visit him and to see what progress he was making. While I was down there I heard an unusual sound. Out in the grassy field next to the garage there was a racket going on.

I stood in front of the garage, which was about ten feet from the edge of the field. We looked out into the field and could see a brown-striped head sticking out of the tall grass. As we watched, an American bittern stood up tall and started making its "oonk-a-choonk" call in a loud voice.

A second later, another bittern started making the same noise from a few feet away. They both hollered at each other for a minute or two, then they started dipping their heads at one another and swaying from side to side. Now this was something we had never seen before!

One would duck down into the grass and then the other would make a few funny moves and the first one would reappear in a different place around the other. They were performing some sort of bizarre dance, which we figured had to have something to do with choosing a mate and bonding. The interesting part was that we could only see tantalizing glimpses of them as they dipped and moved through the tall grass.

All of a sudden, the movement stopped and they both vanished down into the grass. After only a minute or two, one of the bitterns flew straight up into the air. A second later the other one flew up to join it and they both made a beeline right for us!

It was disturbing as they flew in our direction, but they had such eyes for each other and their destination that they must not have even seen us.

Pat and I ducked as they seemed to be aiming for our eyes and they passed over our heads with only a few feet to spare. They ignored us as they flew across the lawn and headed into the deep woods where the swamp was located.

The experience only took a minute but it sure was exciting!

American Bittern

Mother nature prepares for winter

Every September, up north here our evenings begin to cool off and Mother Nature begins to prepare her children for winter. The leaves slowly don their coats of fiery red, coppery yellow, and burnished golden-orange.

The birds begin to prepare by stocking up their seed caches. The blue jays continue to hoard seed, corn and nuts into their hidey holes, while the squirrels and nuthatches steal their ill-gotten booty.

The ruby-throated hummingbirds are feasting fast and furious as they attempt to build up energy reserves for the long flight to Central America. An old theory used to proclaim that "Hummingbird feeders should go out on Memorial Day and be pulled back inside by Labor Day."

That theory no longer holds true. Bird behaviorists claim that we should leave the hummingbird feeders out as long as possible to tide over the late migrants coming through from Canada. Hummingbirds will continue to migrate through our area as late as November and full nectar feeders left out act as a beacon to hummingbirds anywhere along their journey.

Fall is the season for us also to plan ahead for the next growing season and it is time to learn how to take advantage of nature's bounty.

For those of us who are avid gardeners as well as bird-watchers, there are many plants to be ordered for spring and also some to plant yet this fall to attract birds next year. The proper flowers and plants will roll out a welcome mat for many of our winged friends come next spring. The bonus side to these plants is that they also attract those wonderful winged flowers - butterflies.

I was given some Touch-me-not seeds from a friend on Sugar Island and am anxious to plant those. My friend was delighting all summer over the way that the hummingbirds and bumblebees are constantly delving into the tiny tubes of these flowers. His were white and rose-colored but the Touch-me-nots that I have seen growing wild in Barbeau and on Nicolet Road in Sault Ste. Marie are a beautiful orange color with reddish-brown spots.

Without a doubt, my favorite pick of the year is the Butterfly Bush (Buddleia). I planted six of these this spring, each in a different color and I was amazed at their growth! As the flowers began to bloom, many different kinds of butterflies such as Monarchs, Viceroys, Milbert's Tortoiseshells, Sulphurs, Admirals, and Commas began to show up. They came early, stayed long, and lingered to visit each plant.

Keeping to a time schedule of their own were the ruby-throated hummingbirds, who came in by the droves to visit the new plant! Each flower head consisted of at least 50 tiny flowers and I believe the hummingbird stuck her bill into each one for a quick lick. Sometimes she would sit on the flower head while dining, but usually she just hovered. Too darling for words!

Observations

Guess what this is?

• Jan B. from Sault Ste. Marie asked me one day: *"Oh Wise One. Yesterday a white bird tried to get into our house via the dining room window. Didn't get my camera out in time to get a pic, however, it then went to the front door and sat on a chair for a couple of hours. I noticed it had a black type smudge on top of its head and also black on the underside of its tail feathers otherwise it was pure white. Beautiful. There appeared to be a reddish ring around its eyes also. Any idea what kind of bird this is? I can't find it in my bird books."*

Birds high and low

• Bonnie B. from Sault Ste. Marie sent this interesting note along to me: *"I had some bird experiences I wanted to share today. I was surprised to find an owl on the kitchen window sill yesterday late afternoon. I think, by the size, dark eyes, yellow beak, it was a barred owl. I don't believe it hit the window, this is a very protected spot, southern exposure that is warm, overlooking open ground on the south side of the house. If not looking for mice, then maybe red squirrels? Once it noticed my movement, it flew off. I have had something picking off my mourning doves. I assume it is one of the huge hawks I have seen in the area for a couple of months now.*

Also, last month I saw something else interesting. I had been hearing cranes flying overhead all weekend in February but could not see them against the clouds. Finally I got a day with sunny and blue skies. I heard them again, and this time saw three whooping cranes circling overhead way, way up high. With binoculars, you see the white bodies, outstretched necks, and half-black wings. I have seen them before, but not this early!"

Lesson Learned

• Allen D. from Sault Ste. Marie had an interesting shrike story to share: *"Our garage door to the one garage is left open all the time after the snow is gone. Birds get in and get trapped even tho I have opened the side windows. A couple of years ago I came in and found a Shrike fluttering against the window. Many times I have just reached over and carefully cupped my hand around the trapped bird and let it go. I unwitting-*

ly did the same thing with this Shrike. Lesson learned? The little ingrate clamped down on my finger and I had a hell of a time getting it to let ME go. Connie. Let me tell you that these little Passerine hawk types have one hell of a powerful bite for their size. It drew blood and left a welt and it also hurt like hell."

Nesting Owls

• Shirley R. from Drummond Island called one day to share the following: *"About 20 to 25 feet up in a tamarack tree behind our house we have a nesting Great Horned Owl pair. We probably wouldn't have known they were there, but in April and May we heard a lot of hooting and the crows were constantly acting up. Then we noticed some white stuff on the ground at the base of the tree. Once we spotted them, we kept an eye out for them and watched their activities when we could. One of the things we noticed was that 'he' is the decoy to lead people away when they get too snoopy about the nest and that 'she' is much lighter colored than he is."*

Boreal Owl

Duck Tales

• Chris K. from Sault Ste. Marie relates the following stories: *"I wonder if bald eagles in the Eastern U.P. have learned to respond to shotgun blasts like humans would to dinner bells? I was hunting ducks in early November on a partly frozen Munuscong Bay when a nearby party shot a mallard that came down on the ice. While the hunter broke the ice with his boat to get to the bird, a pair of eagles started circling it. One of the eagles picked up the duck twice and dropped it, meanwhile catching the attention of two more eagles. The four were circling and making a lot of noise before the hunter finally retrieved his duck.*

One week later, a friend of mine named Kirk wasn't so lucky. He shot a duck that came down just outside the decoys. Before he could get out of the boat to retrieve it, an eagle came by and snatched it for breakfast. Eagles have been hanging around Kirk since the beginning of the season. On a bluebird day in early October, he shot a mallard on Whitefish Bay after a bald eagle took a dive at a loafing flock of mallards and chased a few of the ducks in his direction..."

A White-tailed Wonder

• From Gene U. of Sault Ste. Marie: *"Each year about this time we have a huge flock of grackles congregating in our yard. We have oak trees and this year there are literally hundreds of acorns on the ground. We saw these birds crack acorns open and pick out the meat. While standing at our window, lo and behold, I saw a white-tailed grackle! It looked so stark among all the black birds.*

It flew up, and then we noticed the under feathers on the tail were black - only the long, top feathers were white! In all the years we have seen grackles, this is a first. I know if I tried to photograph them, they would be startled & fly away, so we just enjoyed watching them."

Chapter Ten

Winter fishing

Occasionally our downstate photographer friend Larry Dech would come up to visit us in the winter. He was looking for great landscape, nature, and wildlife shots. One winter he made a special trip up because he had heard that the great gray owls were here. Great gray owls are a photographer's dream, as they are not afraid of humans and they will sit still for long periods of time, and besides that, they are awake and actively hunting during the day, unlike many other owls.

Larry asked Pat to accompany him while he drove around, as Pat knew the roads around our area much better than Larry did. Pat agreed to go and off the two of them headed early one morning.

As they explored the back roads they found a sitting great gray owl near 9 Mile Road. Larry got out his camera equipment and proceeded to set it up. They did not have the landowner's permission to trek onto his property so they had to set up on the road. When you have the long lens like Dech did, it shouldn't matter anyway. Larry got some great photos, but he wasn't satisfied. "We've got to find a way to get that owl closer to us," he told Pat, "I've got just the thing!" Larry opened up the back of his truck and took out a fishing pole. Then he proceeded to tie what he called an "owl lure" onto the end of the line. Pat said it was gray and fuzzy and he guessed that it looked kind of natural. "It was kinda mouse-looking - whatever it was," Pat said. Little did he know that Larry expected him to be the fisherman!

Dech asked Pat if he would mind doing a little casting out into the field? Pat said he would try it and in the meantime, Larry got his camera all ready for a different kind of shot.

Pat cast out into the field a few times. Then he cast out a few more times. As he was casting he heard a loud noise behind him, and glanced back to see a grader going by on the road behind him. No big deal, they weren't in the way.

A brief thought went through his mind while he was casting, "I hope I don't get ticketed for fishing out of season or I hope they don't know that I don't have a license. Oh well, who's gonna see us?!"

However, no matter how much he cast out into the snowy field, nor where he cast, the owl wouldn't even so much as glance in their direction! After 10 or 15 minutes of trying to get the owl's attention, Pat gave up and told Larry that it wasn't working. He agreed and they packed up their equipment and drove away.

About three weeks later, Pat ran into one of the county guys at a party store down the road. The man asked him, "How's the fishing been lately?" Pat said, "I don't know, couldn't tell you. I haven't been fishing for years!" "That's funny," the guy said, "I know I saw you over on Lechner Road a few weeks ago casting out into an empty field!"

Just when Pat thought nobody had seen him, he remembered the grader that passed behind him and he put two and two together. It was then that he realized that he was probably the subject of conversation at the County garage that night. It's too bad he didn't catch anything, or he would have had a real story for them!

It's time for a Latin lesson

Part of the difficulty with bird watching is that it requires knowledge. Knowledge of names, species, and classification.

Some people gain this knowledge as they age, over a lifetime of birding experiences. Others will pore over birding journals and field guides in a frenzy each time they spy a new bird, in an effort to "cram" names and facts into their subconscious memory.

The ancient Egyptians from the eighth century had the right idea. They used hieroglyphics, or pictures, to identify various birds, such as falcons or hawks. Simple, yes, but not very accurate.

As mankind advanced and expanded into different cultures and languages, the problem with naming birds became more difficult. A solution was devised by a Swedish botanist named Carolus Linnaeus in the 1700s. His idea was to assign a unique scientific name to every living thing, so that it could be used and understood by people of all nationalities. He came up with the idea of using Latin names to classify any organism, because Latin was the language used by scholars at that time.

In Linnaeus' era, classifications of birds were based solely on how they looked - with size, shape, and color being major factors. Now that we've entered a new century, we have realized the many advantages that science has brought to us.

The science of classifying living creatures is called taxonomy and the way that we now label birds has increased in its complexity and accuracy. Taxonomists can now use the biological fields of paleontology, ecology, physiology, behavior, and DNA analysis to help them correctly name birds. DNA analyses have proven to be especially helpful in separating bird species quite precisely.

Yale University reported that two of its researchers, Charles Sibley and Jon Ahlquist, "have resolved many long-standing uncertainties in the field of taxonomy," by using DNA research.

As if the chore of learning hundreds of common bird names isn't enough, scientific research is changing even those names.

Many average bird-watchers could probably care less about the scientific (Latin) names of birds, but instead will concentrate on the common names for the birds that they want to identify.

The scientific names, however, are very useful when identifying birds with the same common name in two languages, which are actually two very different birds. A good example was listed in *The Nature Company Guide to Birding.* They talk about robins in North America, but there are also robins in the United Kingdom and Australia that are very different than the rusty-breast-colored bird which we all know so well here in Michigan.

Even though their common name is the same in three different countries, the three types of robins are not related at all.

Sometimes the Latin names can be fun, even if you do not know Latin. The Eastern kingbird is accurately called the Tyrannus Tyrannus (due to its royally intolerant temperament) and

Eastern Kingbird

Cardinalis Cardinalis is obviously the Northern cardinal.

Don't get too confident though. Pheucticus ludovicianus and Parus atricapillus will still throw you (if you can't guess, they are the rose-breasted grosbeak and the black-capped chickadee).

Suffice it to say that the scientific names are available in any decent field guide if you are interested in learning them. The first word is the genus (group name for related species) and the second word is the specific name. Sometimes a third word will also be included as the subspecies name to throw you off course.

Good luck with the names!

Nest box camera

One of the readers of my weekly birding column gave me a present one day. He said that he had been given a bluebird house with a camera inside it and that he had never used it. Did I want it?

Well of course I did! Pat mounted it on a fencepost at the edge of our property and we ran the video wire to the inside of our garage/workshop. We turned on the attached television and then we waited.

The tree swallows had been back from migration for about a week or so and they were zooming around in the air around the yard eating bugs and whatnot. It wasn't long before they discovered the new nesting box right there in their territory.

One of the swallows would sit on the front of the box, then zip inside to check it out, coming back out a minute or so later. What did it do when it was in there? Measure for carpet?

Pretty soon there were two swallows checking out the box and we knew that it was going to happen - we were going to have some new tenants. It wasn't long and both of the soon-to-be parents were zooming back and forth with grasses of various lengths. It seemed like hundreds of trips were made, and that's just when we were there to watch them!

It became a regular occurrence to see the tree swallows flying around the yard with brown and green grass in their beaks, only to see them disappear into the box opening without even pausing to check for clearance.

When we noticed that they were going into the box we started watching the TV to see what they were doing. It was fascinating! One would haul the building materials while the other spent most of the time arranging them "just so." Within a few days, one of the birds - I assume the female - was sitting on the newly made nest without moving for hours. When she would get up to go out and grab a bite to eat we would be able to count the eggs. First one, then two, then three and soon there were six eggs! Wow! She must really be inspired by the new home!

We couldn't watch the TV monitor all the time, however, as yard work and our jobs interfered. So we watched the mini drama unfold in spurts as we were able to watch them every now and then.

The babies all hatched out within a few days and pretty soon the parents started rotating shifts on the remaining eggs and sitting on top of the youngsters. They must have needed a lot of heat, as mom (or dad!) spent a lot of time squashing them down into the grassy nest. One adult would hunt for a while and then appear at the box opening with a juicy morsel, which was the clue for the other adult to get up and go out to get the next meal. They would awkwardly pass each other in the box, or they would make a "pip" sound before they shot in and the inside adult would vacate first. As soon as that "pip" sound was heard the nestlings mouths shot open instantly and they jockeyed for premium positioning to get fed. The highest and most noticed mouth got the food first.

Amazingly enough, they all got food on an odd sort of rotation and they would step and tramp on one another to get into position for the next round, settling down and sleeping until they heard a noise and then "pop!" up all the heads would come and the mouths would instantly slam open.

The small chicks grew wildly fast and feathers started appearing on their tiny bodies before we knew it. Then their eyes opened and they started to squirm even faster. Mom still came in regularly to sit on them and she would also spend a huge amount of time digging in the nest around the nestlings. We eventually figured out that she was looking for poop sacks which she would grab up in her beak and take out of the nest. When watching from the outside we would see her drop them in the field about 10 feet or so from the nest as she flew away. Every now and then she would get lazy and just eat the poop sacks (gag).

It was like we had a peephole into a fascinating new world that we had never seen before. Just about that time when the chicks were really getting active, we decided to have a garage sale. We left the monitor on during the sale and when the chicks were getting fed, they made very loud peeping noises which would echo through the garage. Many people snapped their heads around to see where the birds in our garage were and they were very intrigued by the drama unfolding there on the TV screen. There were some interesting conversations that day!

During the next few weeks, we watched them as they grew by leaps and bounds. It wasn't long and one at a time they would appear in the nest box hole waiting for their dinner to arrive. While they were inside the box, they would spend time fluttering their wings and would jostle for position by stepping on each others' heads. Occasionally they would scratch itchy spots with their tiny feet or stretch every which way they could. It was a tight fit with six nestlings in there and every ounce of space was taken.

And then one day they were all gone. The parents would hover outside of the box and chatter at them like crazy. One by one the

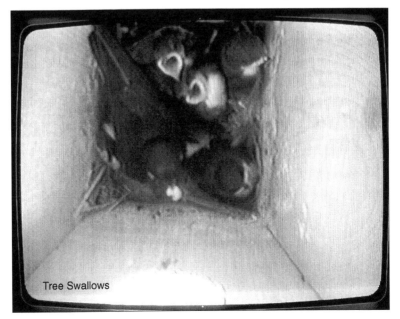

Tree Swallows

chicks would leap out of the hole and snap their wings open and they would vanish into the air of the world.

Our days of bird voyeurism were done until the following year when we would gladly start all over again.

Autumn memories

On one particular fall day, the air was especially crisp and beautiful. The air was shining with the promise of an expected cold winter and many of nature's creatures were frantically bustling about. The leaves from the maple, birch, and oak trees were ablaze with their own respective riotous colors and a lone stately blue spruce stood out in sharp relief against them.

The large tray bird feeder in front of the spruce was freshly replenished with sunflower seed and the activity around it was amazing. Black-capped chickadees, pine siskins, and American goldfinches were flitting to and fro as if they were balls being tossed by a juggler.

The chickadees were carefully selecting only the choicest morsels in their tiny beaks and then were escaping to the safety of a nearby branch to dine at their leisure.

The siskins were bold as they gently searched for broken-open seeds. They hopped about on the tray, munching all the way, stopping here and there to fraternize and bicker with their brothers, sisters and cousins.

Like glimpses of gold among the ore, the goldfinches were jostling one another about on the tray amongst the chickadees. A constant hopscotch of activity was in play as the flock members repeatedly switched positions.

Another feeder hung off to the left, a thistle feeder also recently filled the night before. One by one the finches discovered its delicious contents and started to take position at the perches. A lone pine siskin also ventured over to taste its treats, but he could not find a seat. He resigned himself to running around on the tray below the perches, hoping for thistle seed leftovers to fall his way.

The chirping and twitting of the varied flock rose and fell in frequency as they all fed contentedly. Amidst the chatter - suddenly a distinct high-pitched ZZEEEEEEP! was heard over it all.

An explosion of feathers, feet, and beaks blasted into every direction. Chickadees, finches, and siskins dashed and darted for the shelter of the nearby pine tree, flying at their fastest, and with not a single glance backward.

Right behind the tail of a lagging chickadee a small, wickedly hooked beak appeared, followed by a slim gray, black-and-white body streaking immediately behind.

The fast-paced dance of life and death lasted but a fraction of a second as the frenetic chickadee zipped into the nearest and tightest spruce tree branch opening that it could find.

The pursuing Northern shrike almost flipped backward as it performed a "stop-on-a-dime" maneuver, braking hard in order to keep from crashing into the tree opening where it could not fit.

Frustrated, the shrike uttered a shrill, rasping cry and hovered near the end of the branch, sharp eyes ever alert for the furtive movement of the chickadee within.

Meanwhile, back at the thistle feeder the seed-hunting siskin

Northern Shrike

had become a bird statue. Just as if it were carved in stone, not a feather twitched nor did it move a single muscle. The siskin was hunched close to the feeder and doing its best to blend into the wood.

Ten feet away at the spruce, a new dance had begun. The chickadee, being too frightened to remain still as the shrike peered intently into the gloomy tree, began to flit from branch to branch and from one side of the tree to the other - all while staying inside the protection of the thick branches.

Performing its own moves in a synchronized ballet

with the chickadee was the shrike. It flew up and down, and around and around trying to get close enough to snatch the frantic chickadee.

Still, the siskin remained immobile, drawing no attention to itself at all. Finally, after 10 minutes of the seemingly endless hide-and-seek game, the shrike pushed downward with a strong wing-beat and rose to the top of the spruce. There, it perched (gently) on the top bough, where it resembled a live Christmas tree topper.

Within the spruce, not a peep nor a rustle was heard. There was no more action at the bird feeders and time seemed to stand still for awhile, especially for the siskin sitting alone exposed. Its heart raced and threatened to leap out of its throat, yet even now its eyes slowly scanned the immediate area.

Quicker than a blink, the shrike leaped up and tucked her wings in close for a dive. Straight down towards the close-cut lawn she flew. As the dark shadow passed over it, the siskin seemed to shrink and flatten even more into the bird feeder.

Yet right on by went the shrike, intent on something it had spied at ground level.

SMACK! Feathers and fur mingled for a second as the shrike attacked a small, fat deer mouse from the air. The shrike lingered over her catch for just a minute, getting her footing just so and grasping the mouse more securely in her hooked beak. Then, satisfied that all was secure, she lifted off with her prey, dusting the tops of the weeds on her way across the field.

Two seconds later, a fluttery noise announced the reawakening of the siskin and it hopped up to the first perch on the feeder, sure of its knowledge that everything was all right again and that it had now acquired a prime feeding position.

Within 15 seconds, small-winged bodies began pouring onto the feeders again. It was a gorgeous fall day, the flock was happy and the food was plentiful.

Chimney traps

It seems that folks all around the country often have interesting tales to tell about their chimneys. I imagine that they are a magnet for all kinds of wildlife, as chimneys are easily accessible on the roof.

One day, Daniel L. called to retell an incident that had happened to his father, Jay. Apparently, Jay was too embarrassed to call, so Dan took it upon himself to call me.

One day, Jay was sitting around relaxing when he heard a rustling in the fireplace. They all brushed it off as they thought it was a mouse settling in.

A short while later, when the noise continued they opened up the fireplace to investigate. Jay found a full-grown duck with a rust-colored head and a brownish body in the chimney cleanout.

He gently removed it and took the dirty duck over to the neighbor's house to show them before he let it go.

It was only about a week later that Jean S. sent me the following email: *"I always read your column first in the paper to read about other people's birding experiences. After reading about the duck in the fireplace I just had to report that we had the same thing happen.*

I was cleaning house and heard this noise near the chimney fireplace area. I told my husband about it but we didn't hear any further noise. Then we went into the basement and we both heard an even louder 'bunch of noise.'

We have found bats (old and dried up) that had fallen down the fireplace flue but this was coming from the flue leading from our big basement woodstove.

We had to investigate and get it out of there before we could light the woodstove if we needed to. He disconnected the stove from the ceramic pipe leading to the flue and lo and behold he came up with a duck!

He had used a towel to grab it out but still almost got scratched by the small hooked black nails on the ends of its webbed feet. We took a close look and it had a brown/rust colored head and very golden eyes. He released it safely out the back door and it made a bee-line for Canada and the Garden River that fronts our Sugar Island home.

A neighbor later told us that it might have been a common golden eye duck. That could explain the sharp hooked little black claws... I think some of these ducks roost in trees. This one was probably sitting up on the chimney on the roof and fell over backwards down the flue. And that's my duck story!"

Check out that bird

I am reminded of an interesting event that happened a few years back. Some friends of ours were out bird-watching and they recounted an event in their trip.

It was winter and the birders were out looking for winter birds in the Eastern Upper Peninsula. They were driving around in a caravan of three cars, which were slowly cruising the back country roads and even a few town roads. They had been fairly successful, seeing pine grosbeaks, pine siskins, ruffed and sharp-tailed grouse, along with the usuals like goldfinches, chickadees, and blue jays.

What they were really hoping for were some winter owls, like snowy's, great gray's, or long-eared and short-eared owls. They anxiously looked from side to side and scanned every tree, bush, pole, and fence post for any sign of a bird.

Then the cry was heard, "There's an owl - I think it's a snowy!" All eyes were focused on the pointing hand as the window was rolled down and everyone squinted their eyes to look out over the snow-covered landscape to see what they could. There, a few hundred yards away was a spot of white in the branches of an elm tree. It stood out from the darkness of the tree on the edge of the forest and seemed to move gently from side to side.

A dozen pair of binoculars were brought up and focused on the far-away object. There were a few "oooohs" and "ahhhhs," as people focused on the bird. One person said, "I think it just turned its head - I can see its eyes." Positions were adjusted and a few winter-hardy souls stepped out of the vehicles to get a better look.

Although the owl was a distance away, it was still a consensus that it was a snowy owl, and probably a mature one at that - with all of the white on its body. Everyone seemed to be satisfied, so the optics were packed away and everyone piled back into the vehicles to move on to find the next bird.

Over the course of the day, many birds were added onto the life lists of the participants and it was agreed that the trip had been successful. Pileated woodpeckers, a rare boreal chickadee, and a flock of Bohemian waxwings had been found so everyone was happy.

Just as a last-minute thought, it was decided to go back one more time to see if the snowy owl had gotten any closer to the road for a better view. By now it was approaching dusk and the lighting and shadows were much different than earlier when they had been at that particular spot.

Again the spot of white was seen, but it looked like the owl had not moved at all! "That must be its favorite hunting perch," someone piped up. Again binoculars were brought out and focused on the elusive bird. "Wait a minute..., " a person in a back seat started to say, "That's not an owl! That's a plastic bag!!!"

There were sounds of disbelief and disappointment uttered from every single person. Sure enough, they had spent precious bird-watching minutes looking at a profile of a plastic bag - or what has jokingly been called a California tumbleweed. There was some embarrassed laughing and snorts of disgust at each other, but the incident added a touch of humor to a long day and made it a perfect day of bird-watching.

That's how bird-watching goes... sometimes you see the bird and sometimes you don't!

Observations

Lamprey dinner

• Carol J. from Blissfield wrote a letter one day to report a neat sighting: *"I thought you might find interesting a sighting I had at Mission Point sometime in May. I'm not really a bird watcher — I'm one of those boat nerds that can be found most any time during the shipping season, lined up at Mission Point shooting the same boats over and over.*

I don't care much for little tweety birds, but do enjoy BIG birds - sandhill cranes, herons and eagles. Early into this visit to Mission Point, I watched the Canadian Wildlife and Fisheries crew dump sterile lampreys into the river at the Point. And then I watched the seagulls stuff lampreys down as fast as they could catch them (There were times when I wondered who had who!).

The day after the lampreys were dumped in, we were back at our usual boat watching spot. Suddenly some 25/30 cormorants rose up from the water en masse and were quickly joined by an equal number of seagulls.

What a surprise to see in the center of the squawking birds - a westbound eagle with a lamprey in its beak.

The poor eagle took a lot of hits from swarming gulls and cormorants before it dropped the lamprey and headed back downriver. It was an amazing free-for-all— and there I sat with a 35mm camera and a 70/300 lens beside me on the front seat and a camcorder in the back seat.

No photos — I was just so amazed at what I was seeing, I forgot all about the cameras.

As I said, I don't care much for tweety birds. In our corner of Michigan, about all I see at the feeder are thousands of sparrows and blackbirds.

We have a few robins and an occasional cardinal or bluejay. Boring!! The most excitement I get at my bird feeder is the hawk that thinks I'm running a sparrow buffet restaurant just for him. It bothers me to feed the birds and then cause them to be dinner for the hawk. Ah, but I digress–."

Big Birds

• Jean S. sent along an email with a wonderful big bird sighting day: *"Since our big pileated female brought her mate and showed him the suet feeders he has been a regular visitor with or without her (usually without her). She sort of just appears suddenly but with him it is a different story.*

First you hear him calling from a distance, then you hear a large bump or semi-crash and he is there. He then calls again, drums a little and settles down to eat.

Sometimes she will come in and peck a bit at the suet and fly off. He then will fly off after her and then they'll both settle into a tree for a bit before flying off to wherever ... as a couple. They were both here with him hopping along the railing and stopping to drum a bit before joining her at the suet feeder.

When they are in the hairy woodpeckers stay away. However, I have been noticing that the little downies just shift to the second suet feeder under them and also catch what they drop. Come to think of it one of the little downy guys stay out there when I am filling the seed feeders.

As for other sightings, I saw two juvenile great blue herons perched atop a couple of our big pine trees two days ago. Today it must have been our "big bird" day. Five sandhill cranes flew over very close to the house. Two bald eagle adults came in and perched (they are still there). Earlier an osprey came in and also a juvenile bald eagle flew past very close to the house and perched in a tree closer to the river than where the two adults were sitting. It has been a very interesting day. In the span of one hour I saw three bald eagles, five sandhill cranes, two pileated woodpeckers, three downies, two hairies and one osprey!! You just don't see this in the Detroit area."

Garage Surprise

• Al L. from Kinross sent me this neat note one day: *"I was visiting my parents in Florida a month back and we heard a commotion out in the garage.*

I opened the door and found this bird on the garage door support railing.

I quickly took its picture figuring no one would believe me when I told them this story.

I then reached up and pried its talons off the rail and gently grabbed it by the back and lowered it down. I then let it out the garage door.

The bird was actually quite friendly the whole time as I think it flew into the garage to get away from another bird... its mate was squawking outside something fierce until I freed it from the garage."

Cooper's Hawk

Winter is coming

When winter comes along every year, it is fun to watch the change as it gradually happens. The birds must prepare for winter too in their own way.

It is during that time of year that the cold, stiff breeze blasts the leaves from the trees and sends them dancing into tiny tornadoes down our driveway. That same wind is shouting the words, "Winter is almost here!" into the collective minds of both humans and birds alike. The ruffed grouse in the woods behind our house took on a fluffed-up appearance as they tried to trap some of that last, remaining, warm summer air in their feathers next to their skin.

Ruffed Grouse, male

The resident male was proudly strutting to and fro and dashing from female to female to show them what a prize he was. The hens, of course, were too busy stuffing their beaks with corn and sunflower seed to pay much attention to him.

Just down the trail a little, a woodcock was sunning himself and slowly bobbing his body up and down as he gingerly crossed the gravel. He was not in any hurry at all, because he was just about ready to start his own migration. While the sun was shining though, he didn't feel rushed at all.

The goldfinches were taking a temporary siesta as they completed their second molt of the year. Soon the males and females alike will have donned their winter wear and will blend into the dull brown colors that the local fields and grasses have assumed.

Late fall is a great time of year to check your yard for bird nests. The starkness of the bare tree branches throws the shadowy figures of various bird nests into sharp relief against the steely gray autumn skies. Remember that birds nests can be found high up in the trees. Orioles will construct their sock-like nests as high as 60 feet while rose-breasted grosbeaks will build low, like in a dense bush.

Once the leaves had fallen around here, a few other discoveries were made. The pileated woodpecker and common flicker nest boxes that Pat had made and put up last spring were not used. There was sufficient evidence of excavation, showing that they were at least checked out by some sort of critter.

It is interesting to note, that when observing the common flickers as they excavated their nests, they chose an old snag not more than 15 feet from where Pat put up the nest box. I wonder, is it coincidence or future flicker planning?

We also spied a perfectly round hole near the top of another nearby snag. The hole appeared to have been occupied recently, but neither of us could remember seeing a bird using it. Perhaps the normal summer greenery hid the hole from view until then.

The hummingbirds seemed to have the most sense of all. Many of them have already left by this time of year, heading south to their warm winter homes. You should keep an eye out for the occasional wanderer coming through from Canada though. They may yet need a nectar pick-me-up. Even as the hummingbirds have left us, other birds are gathering together to bravely face the coldness. For example, we recently saw a flock of over 40 sharp-tail grouse. They flew directly in front of us while they crossed from one field to the other.

Maybe the most amazing sight of all was the sandhill cranes. Twice in one month an interesting phenomenon occurred over our house. The event started with only a couple of sandhill cranes circling in the sky above our heads. Then, gradually, a couple at a time flew in to join the ever-expanding circle. The flock continued to increase in number, even as they ascended, until there were over 50 birds in the circling mass. Higher and higher they went, until the wind shifted, carrying them out of sight.

Another new bird sighting that happens in the fall is the appearance of snow buntings. They have been showing up in increasing numbers. One roaming flock I saw had well over 100 birds in it. I saw the roaming flock flitting over a freshly plowed field. When I stopped the truck to get a better count, I was unable to find them. They had vanished between the dirt ruts to search out the exposed weed seed tidbits hidden there.

A few minutes later, when I pulled into our driveway, I discovered two robins foraging in the yard for any sluggish worms they could find. Just as I had myself all prepared mentally for winter, Mother Nature had to go and throw in a few robins to befuddle me.

Bird feeder eater

I'm not sure if I've ever mentioned it or not, but Pat and I spent over a decade on the craft show circuit making and selling different types of bird feeders and bird houses. We had (and still do!) great teamwork - he would build them and I would decorate them. It was much more convoluted than that, but these are the essentials.

When we made our first bird feeders, we used our backyard as our trial ground. It was there that we would try out an idea we had, and where we would see how much the birds liked it or didn't like it. Then we would refine the idea and take it on the road with us. Sometimes our ideas worked, and sometimes they didn't. Weirdly enough, some of our best working bird feeders were the worst selling ones. I guess humans and birds shop differently!

Anyway, many of the bird feeder pictures you see in this book have come from that trial ground in our backyard. Along the way, we have had a tremendous amount of fun and have met some wonderful people.

Simply telling someone that a bird feeder works is one thing, but if you show them a photograph of it working, then that is the selling point! We fashioned a flip book of all of our bird feeders in action. It was so popular that it got worn out and the pages had to be replaced four times!

One day, we were trying out a new type of a round, tall sunflower seed feeder with wire mesh sides. We had some leftover scraps of cedar for which this feeder was a perfect solution. We filled it, hung it outside that day and then went inside to observe any activity.

It was a hit! Almost immediately the chickadees and nuthatches were crawling all over it, right-side-up and upside-down - it

didn't matter to them. We didn't put any perches on the bird feeder, but that didn't seem to matter to them. They could get the seed out just fine and they didn't have any problems grabbing ahold of the wire mesh. Pat and I spent an enjoyable couple of days watching the different types of birds using the new feeder and had decided that this could be a new addition to our product line.

Then, one morning, we looked outside and the new feeder was gone. I don't mean that it had fallen on the ground. No. It wasn't there. Nor was it anywhere that we could see it. It was completely gone.

We have had raccoons

come in from time to time, and they are wreckage kings. With their fat, round bodies they can destroy just about any bird feeder and there isn't much that can be done to stop their rampages. We suspected a raccoon, but if it was the culprit, the bird feeder should be on the ground and opened up by their clever little hands (the same hands that can open toothpaste tubes, peanut butter jars, and cooler lids).

Pat searched for days for that bird feeder and it wasn't anywhere to be found. It had simply vanished! Finally, about the time that he had given up on it, he found it deep in the woods behind our house. Needless to say, something much larger than a raccoon had absconded with it. The bite marks and the way the mesh was crushed so easily led us to believe that a black bear had decided to have some "take-out" that night.

Sometimes you get the bear, and sometimes the bear gets you. I guess we lost that night and needless to say, that idea was scrapped for the time being.

A bird in the hand

Ever since Pat and I have seen pictures of people in magazines with birds on their hands, we have wanted to do the same thing.

It looks simple enough, right? You just go outside and stand

Black-capped Chickadee

real still, then you put some birdseed on your hand and start to play the waiting game. Then you wait and wait and wait.

Sometimes we are successful, sometimes we are not. It appears to be mostly about need. If you are standing among a forest of filled bird feeders, the birds have no reason to even approach you. However, if all of the bird feeders are empty, and you stand out there with a handful of seed, your chances of getting a bird on your hand are pretty good.

I'll never forget my amazement at how it felt the first time that I had a bird land on my hand. Its touch was so light that if I wasn't looking right at the bird, I never would have known that it was there. Of course the intrepid bird that is always the most curious is the black-capped chickadee. When it lands on your hand, all you can feel is the slight pricking sensation of its tiny little toes grasping your fingers. There is no weight at all and usually they grab a quick seed and take off again.

Before any bird will land on your hand, they have to test you first. We find that they usually do a couple of quick "fly-bys" first, buzzing your head or maybe your hand. Then, if you don't move and they don't sense any danger, they might try to grab a quick seed.

Sometimes the birds will surprise you too. Our backyard birds are especially fond of peanut butter. If it has been a cold night, often they will land on our spatula or on the lip of the peanut butter jar while we are filling the peanut butter feeders. It is in this way that they show us how excited they are to be getting some yummy peanut butter which is a lifesaver on cold winter days.

I've watched the chickadee's dive-bomb Pat every now and

Black-capped Chickadee

then when he goes outside to fill the bird feeders. Occasionally they'll land on his hat or on his shoulder, but when he puts out his hand, they ignore him. It's almost like they are cheering him on and encouraging him to move faster, but when he takes a second to acknowledge their presence, they zip off into the trees.

Different species of birds have different levels of "comfortable-ness" around humans. I've seen gray jays and magpies take peanuts and snacks from people's hands with no hesitation at heavily-populated parks and campgrounds. Other birds like woodpeckers and finches wouldn't be caught dead landing on a human and they act like they want nothing to do with us.

If you have a half-hour or so of time to kill and want to give it a shot, all you have to do is cover up your bird feeders and then stand (or sit) outside with some birdseed in your hand and be very still. The braver little souls will spend a lot of time checking you out first, but if you persist, generally you too will eventually hold a tiny bit of fluff in your own hand - even if for only the briefest of seconds. In that short moment of time, you will find that you have been hooked and will try it over and over again!

Chapter Eleven

Crane watching

There is something about cranes that I find fascinating. The common crane for this area is the sandhill crane so, of course, that is the species that I talk about all the time. First of all, it is their calls - so primitive, loud and unique - that I can't get enough of. Then there is the fact that I also love the way they look. They have strange-looking tails, which aren't straight or upright, but instead hang down from their rumps like the bustle on an old-fashioned dress.

Add to that their very long legs and their very long neck and beak and you have an unusual combination of traits that are very striking. The sandhill crane's coloration is nothing to write home about, but the overall gray color is advantageous for blending into the tall weeds where they like to feed. They do have a sort of reddish-brown topknot on their head, but even that is hard to see if they aren't standing in the right position.

I really like to simply watch them, because they are such an unusual bird and different from the usual birds that come to our backyard bird feeders.

They walk with a regal, self-possessed air, almost like they are the mighty kings of their territory and nobody had even think of challenging them! Stately sandhill cranes stalk through the grasses, both short and long, and they don't seem

Sandhill Crane

to care if they are alone or together with a few of their buds.

Watching the sandhill cranes come back in the springtime is a special delight, and I often forget how much I have missed them all winter until I see them again. They will often fly directly over our house on their way to fields beyond and it is neat to watch them from underneath. They fly with their necks stuck straight out and with their legs dragging behind them, so they are a perfectly balanced flying machine. Their strong wings carry them effortlessly through the air and appear to be both short and powerful.

All in all, cranes are an interesting package of feathers and one I never tire of watching.

So many gulls, so little time

During my childhood, certain impressions were locked into my memory. I can remember going to a beach at Lake Fenton with my family as a young child. During these excursions, we always had a great swim with a picnic lunch afterwards. Seagulls were a constant presence while we ate and they invariably left with part of our lunch. We loved to feed them and watch as they cartwheeled in to fight over our meager leftover lunch scraps.

Imagine my surprise when I recently overheard Ken Hopper from the LSSU Biology Department tell a seventh-grader that, "There is no such thing as a seagull!" The point that he was trying to make is that there are many kinds of gulls, such as the ringbilled gull, which is quite common, but that there is no such bird as a "seagull." I have to believe that everyone, including Ken when he was younger, has called gulls "seagulls" at one time or another. It is a common nickname that millions of amateur birders use, even though it is not technically correct for our area.

Only those people who have had instruction in ornithology or have a vested interest in birds would know the proper gull terminology!

National Geographic's Field Guide to the Birds of North America describes gulls as "A large, widespread group, often called seagulls, but many species nest inland."

The Book of North American Birds by Reader's Digest defines this dilemma nicely, "Thanks to its ability to eat almost anything, live almost anywhere, and offer a vigorous defense of the best nesting sites, the Herring Gull has become so ubiquitous that it is what most people mean when they mention a "seagull."" Reader's Digest also mentions that "the term "seagull" is often a misleading one, for many gulls spend much of their lives far from the ocean."

From these descriptions, I would say that Michigan does not have any "seagulls" at all but, instead, we must technically have "lake gulls."

Even as I stand corrected in the use of my "gull" language, one thing stands out in my mind from the past. When I was in Junior High, a certain book was part of our required reading.

That book taught us lessons about learning to believe in ourselves and how to achieve higher goals in life. The book I am referring to is *Jonathan Livingston Seagull*. It was based on a gull who was searching for something. I can't remember what type of gull it was, only the lesson about his journey.

The word "seagull" seems to be a misnomer for our area, as we are not near any "sea," but instead "seagulls" are what we refer to when we see any type of gull. Improper noun usage, maybe, but mention the word "seagull" and everyone knows what kind of birds you are referring to, no matter where you live.

Observations

Fun with Ringnecks

• Al D. from Brimley shared a neat game-bird sighting with us: *"I took this shot with my 300 lens. Could not get any closer. I kept creeping up with my van and this is as close as I could get. Tried walking but no better luck. It never flew, but ran in true pheasant fashion.*

Am very familiar with ringnecks as I am from Northern Indiana and they were very common. As kids, we used to prowl a farm that stacked cornstalks in the old fashioned teepee way. We would go along and shake a corn teepee and every now and then we could hear a pheasant or it flushed and more often than not we would catch it. We had no use for it and we would just release it. It was just a game to us.

This one was on the road that goes to 9 Mile Point to the old coal dock on the bay - just up from the Charlotte River.

I assume, 1) that it is a welfare bird that has moved out from some-one's winter feeding area; 2) It is indeed a ringneck although it looks a bit strange to me. Have not seen one for a good many years."

Ring-necked Pheasant

Eagle power

• Jean S. wrote to share a bird experience that happened to her husband: *"Just wanted to say that last week my husband was getting some things from the car parked in front of the house and was heading down our little driveway to come in the back door when he heard this heavy hoomph, hoomph sound and felt the air pressure against his chest.*

This startled him and he realized it was the huge juvenile bald eagle who was sitting in our big pine near the deck and had just taken off and was halfway down to the ground flapping its huge wings mightily to get some lift. This eagle has been coming closer and closer to the house. I wonder if it is scouting out our birds for a quick snack???? Or is our tall 'bird tree' a convenient seat to view the river??? He/she has been hang-ing around here although we don't see it every day."

A Slinky Solution

• Janice K. also wrote, but to share some great bird feeding tips: *"As I hope you can see in the photo, I have tried both these ideas, they both work.*

First I was not too happy with the masked bandit that kept knocking the plastic finch feeder down - eventually breaking it. Raccoons are so hard on plastic! I had read about someone using a pantyhose leg, so I thought I would try it. It works great! If it gets a hole, then just tie the bottom knot a bit higher as I have done. The seed never get wet and has to be cleaned out of the 'bottom' of the feeder, the birds clean it out. The hose expands to hold a lot of seed at once, too! It is a challenge to hold it steady as you fill it, but that was solved by setting it inside a bucket which catches the loose seed, also. If there are runs in the stocking, no problem... that's where the finches prefer to pull the seed! It gives them a head start - they don't have to work as hard to remove the seeds.

The second problem I had was a squirrel that scampered up the metal shepherd's hook like it was a tree. It was in the feeder constantly and the birds didn't have a chance - or the sunflower seeds were gone. I read about another birder who used a Slinky to discourage a squirrel from climbing the pole - it works! As the squirrel tried to climb, the Slinky moved and the squirrel fell back to the ground.

I thought these ideas might come in handy for others with the same problems..."

Suet-making time

I once informed a bird-feeding friend of mine that it was time to put suet out for the birds. She glanced at me curiously and said, "Soo what?" I explained, "You know, that fatty stuff that you can get from the butcher?" After I had finished recoiling from the thoroughly disgusted expression on her face, I figured a proper explanation was in order.

Essentially suet is raw beef fat (or pork) which is found around the kidneys and loins. Many items can be made from it, such as Christmas puddings, gravies, and candles. Many kinds of birds find suet irresistible and it helps to build up their energy reserves so that they can stay warm during cold winter evenings.

By putting out suet, you can attract woodpeckers, nuthatches, robins, bluebirds, chickadees, creepers, wrens, thrushes, kinglets, warblers, and tanagers.

While doing some research on suet, I found over 50 different ways to make it. Popular names for homemade suet are Bird Cakes or Bird Puddings.

Suet can be bought commercially as a premade product, and sometimes it also comes with its own container (either a wire cage or a simple hanging bag). In my own experience, I have never had much luck with commercial brands. The birds usually ignore it until it rots and falls to the ground, much to the delight of the raccoons, bears and squirrels.

The manufacturer tempts us with wonderful names and great-sounding ingredients in their suet cakes, but often the birds prefer homemade or fresh suet.

While I was reading an issue of *Wild Bird,* I read a letter from a lady in New Jersey. She commented that the birds at her feeders absolutely will not touch the commercial brands of suet either and that she mixes them with her own homemade mixture.

If you're not in the mood to mess up your kitchen, the easiest way to put out suet is to simply get suet scraps from a local butcher and hang them outside in a used onion or potato bag. If you know any successful deer hunters, ask them to save the suet from the deer carcasses. Remember to hang it high enough so that any local dogs can't jump up to get it.

A few winters ago, Pat and I were shocked to discover wolf tracks under our suet feeder. Not only had the wolf leaped up and torn it down, it had proceeded to gnaw and chew the feeder apart to get at the goodies.

The visiting bear that we had seen hanging around all summer had an easier answer to the suet problem: it simply ripped the branch off the tree where the suet was hanging and hauled the feeder off into the woods, never to be seen again.

If you are a bit more adventurous and have some time on your hands, making your own suet cakes is easy and rewarding.

1) Melt the suet scraps down, either in the microwave or on the stovetop.

2) Skim off any impurities or else strain the liquid through some cheesecloth or a coffee filter.

3) Let it cool completely, while you gather up some extra ingredients.

4) Any of the following ingredients can be added to suet, at your discretion: peanuts, cornmeal, raisins, oatmeal, peanut butter, berries, sunflower seed, millet, cracked corn, raw coconut, flour, apples, ground-up eggshells, dry cereal, dog biscuits, or watermelon pulp.

5) After the suet has cooled, melt it down a second time. This remelting helps to harden the suet and your extra ingredients should be added when the suet is partially cooled so that they don't float to the top. After remelting a second time, the suet is now considered "rendered suet."

6) After adding the ingredients, pour your suet into whatever containers suit your fancy (paper-lined muffin tins, aluminum foil pans, throwaway plastic leftover containers, etc.), then freeze your mixture until ready to use.

Some people like to spread suet onto pine cones or stuff it into the nooks and crannies of trees or branches. The use of a pastry bag (or a plastic sandwich bag with a corner cut off) during this process saves quite a mess.

Making suet for the birds is a great wintertime project for the whole family and it reaps multiple rewards each time the birds come in to eat from your newly-made suet!

A bird in distress

One day, a gentleman that lived down south of the Rock Cut on the St. Marys River called me. He found an immature osprey huddled down in the rocks on the waterfront side of his property. He asked if I could come down and do something with it.

This man (I'm sorry - I don't remember his name!!! I'll call him Mr. X) had found the osprey hunkered down in the rocks and felt sorry for it. It was so weak and hungry that it allowed him to pick it up and bring it up to the house. He put it in a box and was trying to get it to eat when he called me. He had not been having any luck getting the bird interested in any food, so he called me to see if I knew what to do.

I went over to his house and took a look at the osprey. Oh my goodness, it was so beautiful. It had been banded at one time and sported a bright red leg band. The bird was full grown, but still had some down feathers on its head. It was also weak, timid, and not afraid of us one bit. I could tell right away that it was in serious trouble. Mr. X had been trying to feed the bird frozen smelt that he took out of his freezer, but it wouldn't eat at all.

I lightly grabbed the bird and felt its chest. The breastbone was prominent - which is a strong sign of starvation. I knew we had to

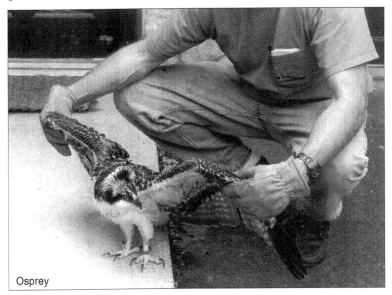

Osprey

do something immediately. We put the bird into a cardboard box to calm it and I called Anne Trissell.

I drove the osprey over to her house and she took a look at the bird. We both agreed on the diagnosis - it needed to eat. She was worried because it wasn't even showing any sign of interest in the food offered to it.

Anne called me the next day. She had force fed the osprey some blended fish scraps and some water. However, it still showed little to no interest in the food, even when she forced the food down its throat.

The next morning the bird was dead. Apparently, the young osprey had not had any success in finding its own meals since it had fledged from the nest. Sometimes, nature is cruel in its design and there is nothing we can do to stop the inevitable.

Preparing for the cold

Imagine waking up one brisk winter morning and discovering that Mother Nature had blessed your yard with a fresh, new blanket of snow. While it may have been beautiful, the drop in temperature and the snow covering the ground poses a serious problem for birds.

How can such a small creature, with only a few thousand feathers, survive the frigid temperatures and cold winds?

During these harsh conditions, birds survive by perching quietly to save energy. They sit with their feathers all fluffed out, conserving and trapping their body warmth within those feathers. The more body fat that they are able to build up in the fall, the better off they will be. That body fat acts like gas for an engine. Once their "gas" is used up they will either starve or freeze to death.

There are differing opinions about bird-feeding pros and cons. Many experts claim that birds do not need the food in bird feeders to survive the winter. A researcher in Wisconsin found that birds will use bird feeders for less than 25 percent of their daily intake. Yet those same experts will admit that any advantage the birds can use during wintertime will increase their survival rates.

Inevitably this means that any birds which can "top off their tanks" at the bird feeders will invariably put on a tiny bit more fat and survive longer.

Some ornithologists have gone so far as to claim that bird feeding benefits humans more than it does the birds. The only benefit that I have found is the enjoyment from watching birds and their antics. It certainly does not benefit my pocketbook, but watching the birds frolic and dart about on a cold winter day, oblivious to the below-zero temperature, is payment enough for me.

Birds in the Upper Peninsula may become slightly dependent on well-stocked bird feeders during unusually heavy snows and especially ice storms, when their natural food sources are ice-locked. Don't worry though, studies have shown that no bird will ever rely entirely on a single source of food, no matter how wonderful it is.

Here are a few tips for winter bird feeding:

1) Make sure the birds can get in to your feeders and keep the seed dry. Putting out bird seed is no good if the birds can't find it. Before any upcoming storms, make sure that all your bird feeders are well-stocked. If you use platform feeders, make sure that they are swept off and replenished after any storms. A quick toss of seed onto the top of a snowbank works well for the ground feeders like sparrows, doves, juncos and, especially, the snow buntings.

2) Provide food in sheltered areas. Quite often, during our Michigan winters, we will encounter day after day of blowing snow. At times, this can make it hard to maintain that trail out to the bird feeders and back. Sometimes, I wonder if I shouldn't leave a trail of bread crumbs to find my way back to the house again! I knew one clever person who solved that problem. They constructed a feeding tube out of PVC pipe. It ran from a window in the house to the bird feeder, with a bit of a decline to the feeder. The person opened the window, poured some seed into the pipe, and voila! The bird feeder had seed in it!

When drifting snow becomes a problem, try to construct a sheltered area in your yard where a windbreak could be beneficial to the birds. A few pieces of scrap plywood or a heavy cardboard box can be propped up to let the snow build up on the back side. Then you can spread seed onto the protected area in the front. After

Christmas is over, a leftover Christmas tree provides an ideal shelter or windbreak when laid on its side.

If you can't do any of these things, then consider simply scattering some seeds under your deck, under some bushes, or along the edge of a wooded area for the shy birds who won't come in to a bird feeder.

3) Provide water, preferably warmed with a birdbath heater. When frost seals off the water and the snow turns it to slush, the birds have no alternative left for drinking water. Any water we can provide could be a valuable resource. Birds do not choose to eat snow unless they have to because it uses up some of their valuable energy to melt it in their bodies, then warm themselves back up again.

Believe it or not, birds also need to bathe and preen themselves during the winter. Their feathers must be kept in perfect shape all of the time so that their insulating properties remain intact. The only thing that should be avoided is deep water in the bird baths. If your water is over an inch deep, then place a few stones or sticks in the water so that the birds can reach down without taking a chance on falling in.

If you can afford a birdbath heater, these are wonderful additions to the bad weather arsenal. Hardware experts tell me that they use no more electricity than a light bulb.

4) Provide high-energy foods. One of the best winter foods that you can provide is suet. Meat scraps and peanut butter are also wonderful energy boosters. Eating these foods allows the birds to gear up for cold winter weather quickly and efficiently, without wasting time cracking open seeds.

5) Insulate your bird houses. I once opened up one of our bluebird houses in the winter, only to discover that it contained quite a bit of bird feces. I actually got excited over this, because it means that some bird in our yard was using the box to roost in every evening to stay warm.

It helps to put some kind of insulating material in the boxes to keep out the cold. Three or four inches of wood shavings or dried grass work well. Put it into your bird-nesting boxes after the last bird has fledged out in the fall. Watch for daytime activity though, as squirrels will also use these boxes as comfy winter snooze boxes, then make nests in them in the early spring.

6) Be ready for big winter changes. Nothing is more disconcerting than to wake up to a foot or two of fresh snow in the morning. Even more upsetting is when the birds come cheerfully down to your feeders to feed, only to find ... nothing. It seems as if the birds look at me so pitifully when this happens and I feel terrible pangs of guilt when I discover that I forgot to buy bird seed the day before.

Amazingly enough, black-capped chickadees require 150 sunflower seeds (or the equivalent in a different type of seed) each day to keep up their energy needs. That number increases to 250 seeds per day in a severe storm.

Every year 30 million tons of seed is put out for the birds in North America. Some of my friends tell me that it seems as if they have bought a few million of those themselves. Sound familiar?

A flood of horror

One spring we were having an exceptional amount of rain. During the course of one week in April, it seemed like it rained every day. Along the dirt road that we live on, there is a small creek with a giant drainage ditch at the road. Most of the time, the size of the drainage pipe is a joke, as School Creek is just a trickle that runs through it.

However, in the spring the snow melts like crazy and the water really gets rolling down the fields and it dumps into the creek.

Pat and I just happened to be on hand one spring to witness an awful event.

We were coming back from town one day and were driving down our dirt road when we noticed a commotion in the hay fields. The water was blasting through the culvert under the road and it was so heavy that the nearby fields were flooded. The snow had melted weeks before but the heavy rains had re-saturated the fields. It was wet everywhere we looked.

The red-winged blackbirds had came back from migration early that year and had already built nests in the grasses. As we were looking out into the field, we saw dozens of gulls hovering over the fields. It was hard to figure out what was going on, as there was such a commotion. The gulls were dipping down and then dipping down again. At the same time, the red-winged blackbirds were coming up to meet them from deep down in the grass. There were clashes between the large, long-winged gulls and the short-bodied black birds.

We stopped the truck to watch the fights - that is, until we realized what was really going on. The gulls had initiated a raid on the red-winged blackbirds' nests. They had come in like an army and started zeroing in on the blackbirds sitting on nests down in the grasses - which were now floating on top of the water. From their aerial view, the birds were easy to see.

The gulls would dip down and draw the attention of the adults, which would then rise up to fight them. Then the gulls would ignore them and dip down again to grab a chick or an egg, whichever was easiest.

We watched in horror as the blackbirds nests' were decimated and the gulls flew off with dozens of chicks in their beaks. We knew that there was nothing we could do, and we slowly drove off to let nature take its course.

Freezer yummies

One winter we were well prepared. We had bought our bird seed for the winter and had put it into two 50-gallon garbage cans stored inside an old freezer in our backyard. From there, we could easily fill the bird feeders and it would be safe from any of the critters with it being inside the freezer. When we had left out garbage cans in the past, the mice had always found a way to chew through the lid or else the raccoons had just plain lifted the lid off. This was our newest solution and we were confident that it would work just fine.

One weekend we took off downstate to attend a craft show. When we got home three days later, we were greeted by a disgusting sight. Our heavy-duty chest freezer had been tipped over! Not only that, but it had tipped over just right so that the contents of both garbage cans had spilled out onto the ground and 100 pounds of corn and black-oil sunflower seed were gone! We were very upset, not only at the loss of a chunk of our income, but also at the pigginess of what could only have been a bear.

Determined not to be outsmarted, we bought more seed (!) and Pat proceeded to make the freezer bear-proof. We were not going to let a fat bear rob our birds of bird seed this winter! Because it was an old freezer, it could not be locked, so he wrapped a heavy length of chain around the freezer to keep it shut, then for good measure he also wrapped the chain around a nearby tree. We were both satisfied that this would take care of the problem.

A few nights after that, I was awakened by a deep, rumbling booming sound. I sat up in bed, wondering what that noise could be. "Booom!" "Booom!" "Booom!" Finally, I woke up Pat, because I really couldn't figure out what could be making such a strange noise that reverberated through our house.

We grabbed up flashlights and went through the house shining our lights through all the windows looking for the source of the booming. Arrgh! When Pat shined his light into the backyard by the freezer, there was a giant black bear! It was standing up on its hind paws and it was trying to push over the freezer! It tried and it tried to do what it had done last time - namely, push on the top of the freezer to tip it over and get at the goodies. The bear just knew that there was something yummy in there!

The booming sound came from when the bear would push the freezer up against the tree each time. Finally the bear stopped for a minute, went down on all four paws, and pondered what to do. Then it began a new tactic. It put its head against the freezer and proceeded to push it with all its might. Of course, nothing happened. A second try saw the freezer move a little bit. Now the bear was encouraged. It pushed and it pushed until it started the freezer moving. However, because the freezer was chained to the tree, all it did was push the freezer around the tree.

Pat finally decided that he had had enough. Pretty soon the freezer would be damaged beyond repair. He grabbed up a rifle and stepped out onto the back porch. He shouted at the bear. It just looked at him. Then he placed a shot just over the bear's head. Now that got its attention! A second shot got him moving.

The bear took off on a lazy ramble from the backyard. Since that night, we haven't heard any more booming noises. And yes, the birds were able to eat all winter on our stored seed.

Observations

One day, during a cold winter morning, a group of bird-watchers from downstate stopped by our house to see what they could find. Usually these groups will be a mixed bunch of men and women of all ages. This time, however, there was a young boy with his parents and he was one of the most enthusiastic people in the birding group. He excitedly told Pat and I about the flock of turkeys they had seen just before coming into our yard and he was jumping up and down when they saw a turkey come into our backyard from the woods.

As something fun to do, I gave the boy a turkey tail feather out of my collection in the garage. He thanked me, and was thrilled to have a "souvenir" from his trip. I told him that I would also send him some turkey wing feathers if he would leave me his address, which he did (I wanted to sort through my feathers and find a couple of nicer-looking ones).

I mailed the feathers out a few days later and received the following letter a few months later:

"Dear Connie,

Alex was so thrilled to receive your beautiful turkey feathers in the mail!! He immediately taped them to his arms and flapped around the yard! :-)

They are now taped to his toy red-tailed hawk.

The bird feeders we purchased from you have been such a treat for our yard! Last week we had over 20 blue jays at one time! We

Cedar Waxwing (Bombycilla cedrorurm)

What color is it?

were so excited!

I hope you are selling oodles of bird houses during this busy time of year!

Thank you for your kindness to our bird-loving 5-year-old!

Your friends 'down south,' Alex & Becca B."

Great Vantage Point

• Dale F. from Sault Ste. Marie sent along a neat owl photo:

Barred Owl and Wild Turkeys

"Feel free to use the pictures if you wish. The owl was sitting over in a maple tree watching the goings on of the other birds at the feeder. He must not eat turkeys, they are still safe. They are all ignoring him now. It has been several years since we have had an owl in the backyard, the last was a great gray. Later the little guy moved over to sit in the bird feeder. Thought you would enjoy a picture of him."

Front Porch Living

• Charlotte T., a member of the Bay de Noc Audubon Naturalists Club, relayed the following: *"We all share a passion - birds, and we refer to ourselves as 'birders,' and to our common commitment as 'birding.' We once spent a year living with a sandhill crane. We didn't adopt that bird as much as the bird adopted us. It lived on our front porch for a year. That was back in the '50s and we had a ball. My husband was with the Forest Service then, and he was interested too. We wanted to know more about cranes and were hoping to hatch one from an egg. Then we found out we could get an adult crane from a sanctuary in Baraboo (WI). The crane eventually came to accept people and became so thoroughly socialized that it would run out to greet visitors, which was an alarming event because of the bird's size."*

Listening First

• In the spring of 2001, James R. from Kincheloe sent the following: *"I was out on a Sunday sitting on my patio in the glorious sunshine. There was no wind. Rather than looking first, I listened first. I heard seagulls and found them high overhead, white silhouetted against a clear blue sky. I heard snow buntings, their quick chirps and the flash of their black-tipped wings. A crow caws in the distance. A pair of starlings replaces the snow buntings and entertains me with a variety of calls. Finally, pigeons are behind me on the telephone wire cooing and waiting for me to vacate the vicinity of the feeders. Spring is coming!"*

Highway Crossing

• From Marty G. also that same spring: *"I love watching birds and of course which means I read your stories every week. I was surprised not to see any word on Sandhill cranes this week? I was heading south on I-75 one morning and a sandhill crossed the highway in front of me! All I could do is laugh thinking it must have got lost in the jet stream! As I got further south, I realized that there was no snow and that they must already be nesting down there. Aren't U.P. winters a blast????"*

Pileated Woodpecker

Silly Robin

• One more spring letter - this one from Jennifer O.: *"I live on M-28 near the intersection of 221 and 28. All winter we have had all three of the woodpeckers - Pileated, Hairy and Downy, visit our yard. I even managed to get* some pictures of the pileated. We have also had a small flock of Sharp Tails that have visited off and on all winter long. I have also counted as many as three dozen mourning doves at one time visiting our feeders. And on Friday at the Brimley VFW Club a brave Robin was looking around for some food. I bet he is wishing he stayed south a little longer with the latest cold wave."

Family Watching

• Glenn L. from St. Ignace sent along this note: "*Everything is out today. Three gray squirrels and one black and two red. The birds are hitting all the feeders. Two pigeons and a couple of mourning doves picking off the ground. The feeders are about ten to fifteen feet from our kitchen windows. Right now a pileated woodpecker is hitting on all my feeders. His crown is bright red and he is over a foot tall... one feeder he is upside-down on - the bowl-covered one on a clothesline - and eating sunflower seeds. Then he is hanging on my regular straight-hanging feeder and reaching over and his tongue comes out for the suet sitting next to it. We are close enough to see his tongue. Then off to a house-shaped feeder as he reaches around and eats sunflower seeds. It is noon and he has been here about a half-hour so far. The goldfinches and starlings were here earlier. My one-year-old grand-daughter is just sitting watching and enjoying the spectacle with us.*"

The great gray ghost

One especially crisp winter morning, I was sitting at my kitchen table eating breakfast when I saw a furtive movement out of the corner of my eye. I glanced out the window, when suddenly I saw it again. It was a field mouse, braving his very life to dash across the driveway in two short bursts of speed. In the blink of an eye, he was back to safety once again.

That quick flash of mouse reminded me of a similar mouse-watcher that I had seen years ago. At that time it was deep winter, the day was full of sunshine and the snow was sparkling with millions of tiny diamonds. I was wandering around in the house in my pajamas and was looking through the windows at the beautiful day.

I glanced down at the woods at the edge of our front yard and saw a shape there that I didn't recognize. It really wasn't too far from where the mouse had run across the driveway. I quickly grabbed up a pair of binoculars and focused on the shape. I was pleased to see that it was a great gray owl. I have a special love for these owls, due to the fact that they are unusual to see in Michigan and also that they are so human-friendly. They never seem to be afraid of us, and often ignore whatever we are doing so that they can continue looking for their dinner.

This particular owl was doing just that. He had his head cocked down and was watching the snowbanks underneath him for rodent activity. All morning long, I had seen mice coming up out of the snow to grab quick snatches of sunflower seed from the top of the snow under our bird feeders.

Just under the tree where the owl was, there was a bird feeder there at the edge of the woods. I'm sure the mice were quite active there as well. Here was my opportunity to watch a great gray owl up close.

Many nicknames sprang to mind for this bird that I only had seen once or twice in my lifetime. They have been called the Great Gray Ghost, Sooty Owl, Ghost of the North, Spectral Owl, Bearded Owl, Spruce Owl, and the Phantom of the North. While I watched, the owl turned its head from side to side and all around to adjust its hearing. Obviously, it had seen or heard the mice or else it wouldn't have been hanging around there. I found that interesting, because I don't know how it could hear anything. The black-capped chickadees were buzzing the owl by flying by close to it and they were calling back and forth to each other while sitting on limbs all around the gigantic owl.

I slipped on my coat and boots and was able to go outside, walk across the yard, and stand next to the tree where the owl was at. It glanced briefly at me, then continued looking elsewhere. The owl was only about five feet above me in the tree! He was regal and beautiful and he allowed me several minutes of picture-taking before he departed. Apparently I was scaring away his meals.

The Great Gray Owl is not a regular visitor to Michigan. Most years they do not appear at all, but every three to five years Mother Nature "crashes" their prey numbers in the subalpine and northern conifer forests of the world.

This sends the great grays packing temporarily to visit us in the Eastern Upper Peninsula. They are not considered a migrant through Michigan, but rather a "visitor" or "nomad." When they are sighted in great numbers, it is considered an "invasion" or an "irruption" year. The biggest invasion was in the winter of 1991-92, when over 60 Great Gray Owls were present in the Eastern Upper Peninsula. When they do appear, their concentrations seem to be highest around Sault Ste. Marie, Neebish Island, and Sugar Island.

The Great Gray Owl is easily identifiable by their large size of 24 to 32 inches and an enormous wingspan of almost five feet. It is a graceful flier despite its large size and they are North America's largest owl, though not its heaviest. I can always tell a great gray by the white "mustache" that they sport just under their beak along with a little black "bow tie."

The great gray is aptly named, as it is overall gray-colored, mottled with little bits of light gray, white and brown. It has a large facial disc, which makes its yellow eyes appear quite small. Also, they lack the ear tufts that many owls have.

This Ghost of the North is also a deceiver. It is a true bird of the northern country and is well-suited to the chilly temperatures there. Its feathers are dense and it has thick insulating down. All these factors contribute to the fact that they are a HUGE bird. But, the heaviest Great Gray Owl only weighs about three pounds, less than half the weight of an adult snowy owl. They are all fluff, but are efficient hunters.

When the ground is covered with snow, the great gray can hunt by hearing alone and will often punch through snow as deep at 12 inches to reach the retreating rodents. Usually the Ghost of the North prefers to hunt from a stationary perch, swiveling its large head around to capture sounds beyond our human hearing.

I affectionately named our Great Gray Owl ,"Hootie," and saw it often in the following weeks. It was not afraid of me at all, and let me approach every time to take superb photographs.

Great Gray Owls have little human contact in the remote northern wilderness areas which are their home and therefore have not learned any fear of humans.

Keep your fingers crossed. An invasion year can happen at any-time. That is the time that I will reach for that list that I keep which has the names of all the people that I have to call. The names of all the people that want to drive up north to see a rarity - a bird that many yearn to put on their life list - the Sooty Owl.

Great Gray Owl

Chapter Twelve

Living room surprise

One day near dusk, Pat and I were sitting quietly in our living room watching television. It was a calm evening and we were content with snacks in our laps and a good show to watch. Our cat, Pheebee, was also content as she napped on top of my recliner and we were all just kicking back relaxing.

All of a sudden, BOOOM! Our world exploded in a shower of flying glass pieces!! Pat and I just looked at each other - we were in shock! What had just happened?! Our glass living room window had imploded around us and we were sitting there with chunks of it in our laps. Pheebee had blasted straight upward off the top of the chair in her surprise and had zoomed off down the hallway before we could even react. I don't think she touched the ground for about ten feet while in her flight mode.

Pat and I sat for a second or so in our surprised stupor before we realized that there was a large flapping creature with us in the living room! I jumped up and said, "Hey! There's a bird in here!" By this time we could see it clearly as it ran out from under Pat's armchair - it was a ruffed grouse! It was flapping like crazy in its extremely agitated state and was trying to look for a way to get back outside. It flew/skipped back over to another window and was futilely thumping against it trying to get outside.

"We've gotta get it before it breaks another window!" I said. Pat jumped up and was at the window in two giant strides. He grabbed up the grouse in his big hands and hustled over to the other side of the house with it. Meanwhile, I was flitting around him, seeing what he was going to do. Pheebee was long gone, of course, hiding under a piece of furniture somewhere in another room with her wits half scared out of her.

I opened the front door and Pat gave the grouse a mighty heave into the air. We had no idea if it was injured or what - we just knew we wanted it OUT of the house! The grouse disappeared in a mighty flurry of wings, but not before blasting through a large bush alongside our sidewalk. It broke many of the bush's branches in its hurry to get someplace safe, but at that point we didn't care. We were both in wonder that the grouse was alive and flying at all.

Pat closed the door and we surveyed the damage. One large, double-paned window lay shattered in various sized pieces all over the living room. We had a clear view to our backyard and the temperature was hovering right around freezing. We started to scramble around to figure out a way to close the new opening and pick up the glass.

What a powerful bird that was to be able to shatter the glass so easily without hurting itself! We could find no blood anywhere, only a few feathers here and there. The only scenario we could picture was that the grouse was flying through the forest at a high rate of speed and didn't see the window in its way. All we knew was that we were going to find glass in strange places for the next few months.

Keeping out those pesky squirrels

One week I had a chance to "talk birds" with a large group of people and there seemed to be a common complaint among the bird-feeding crowd. It was, "How do I keep the squirrels out of my bird feeders?!" I explained to them that if I knew the sure-fire answer to that question, I would be America's next millionaire.

Indeed, I have watched many friends and family in their efforts battling the "furry ones," and there never seems to be a simple answer. Some bird feeders prefer to use funnel-shaped baffles on their posts, or baffles suspended above the feeder to prevent attack from the air. These baffles can take the shape of anything from a garbage can lid or a hubcap to a five-gallon bucket. While buckets are not exactly aesthetically pleasing, they will usually do the trick. Beautification can come later after success has been achieved. Keeping in mind that squirrels can jump an average of eight feet horizontally and about four feet vertically, it is also not wise to place your bird feeder very close to any tree.

One thing we have to remember is that squirrels have been growing up, generation after generation, with one goal in their lives: eating. To their manner of thinking, those seed feeders were put out especially for them - all they have to do is figure out the challenge of getting to them. A squirrel's very existence depends on its being able to figure out how to get to that seed, so it is reasonable to assume that it will do everything it can to get at it.

A few years ago the "hot" item of the year was the use of a new product called Squirrel Away. Basically it consisted of a secret ingredient used to repel squirrels (and probably some humans too). That ingredient was Capsicum, the essence of hot chili peppers. The hope was that the squirrel would eat some seed, get a "hot" mouth and take off quickly seeking water, never to return again.

This strategy worked quite well for some folks. Then again, other people told me that they must have had a strain of Spanish-American squirrels move into their neighborhood, as the squirrels couldn't get enough of the stuff! The manufacturer claimed that it did not affect the birds at all, and that it even had two vitamins in it that the birds needed in their daily diet!

Another interesting idea that someone came up with was this: suspend your bird feeder from a clothesline or between two wires, then string a few 2-liter bottles lengthwise along its length, a few on each side. This creates a barrel-rolling effect when the furry guys walk the wire and then proceed to crawl over the bottle barriers. Whoops. Off they go! I have seen this concept work well. Again, not aesthetically pleasing, but it does the job.

Many bird-feeding people have gone so far as to purchase the all-metal feeders that claim to be "squirrel-proof." The concept that these feeders are built around is a spring-loaded trap door. When a bird lands on the tray to eat, their weight is too slight to set off the spring and they can eat. But let a heavier animal (like a squirrel) or a larger bird (like a crow) land on the tray, and the weight sets off the spring, effectively closing off the feeder entrance.

This is a fine and dandy idea, except for one problem. Remember that the squirrel will do anything that he can do to get to the seed. Quite a few squirrels have been seen cooperating in this particular venture, as they will take turns jumping at the feeder, thereby knocking any seeds to the ground before the trap door swings shut.

Another interesting method that they have learned is to hold on to the top of the feeder with their back feet, then ssstttttrrrrretching around the feeder roof to reach the seed below, without ever touching the tray. Clever, eh? Squirrel-proof? I don't think so.

One other method of discouraging critters is to grease the pole holding your bird feeder. Some people would use different types of grease or automobile oil for this purpose. The end result was that the squirrels would try to climb the pole over and over, until finally they wore the grease off the pole and up they would go - stained bellies and all.

In a similar vein of thinking, other people would use Vaseline or cooking oil, but the furry ones liked the taste of that and would lick it off of themselves in between climbs up the pole.

The last thing you want to do is feed them exotic foods, right?

Observations

A Beautiful Golden

• From Tom P. in Brimley: *"I thought I would drop you a note to let you know we saw a Golden Eagle in a field on the west side of Bound Road at about 6:30 p.m. The bird was on the ground about 100-150 yrds. from the road. It flew after I whistled at it for a while. It was probably the biggest bird I have ever seen.*

After I looked the eagle up in my bird book this morning, I studied up on the rest of the hawks, falcons, etc. When I sat down to write this email I saw a flash of movement out the window. A bird flying off with another bird in its talons. Turned out to be a merlin with a dove. My wife and I went out and watched him with our binoculars for a few minutes. I'm glad he didn't eat one of our sharptail."

Sharptail Squabbles

• From Kitty S. in Stalwart: *"Bob and I always enjoy your articles in the paper as we are bird watchers. We have fed birds for years and try to identify all the birds we see. Last March we put in a big window in our dinette so we can sit at the table and watch the birds at the feeders and under them or in the big maple tree.*

We especially enjoy our big flock of sharptail grouse, we have had as many as 34 at one time, but usually 20 to 24. Bob goes out first thing when he gets up and puts food out for them. Sometimes we feel they must be watching for him as they are there by the time he gets back in the house. We love to watch them. Some are so greedy and so mean to others. They chase each other and scold.

We noticed they often just all took off at once and couldn't understand what would scare them. Then one day I saw a large bird, gray white underneath, brown edge wings, wide wing spread, which we figured was either a large hawk or an owl.

Apparently that is what scares them. But they are soon back and they come up off and on all day.

We also have a pair of pheasants that come in almost every day and feed with the sharptails. Sometimes they will come in 2 or 3 times a day. The hen pheasant is very bossy! They seem to be living out in the trees along our driveway.

One unusual bird we have is a brown thrasher which has stayed here all winter. We see him at the feeders almost everyday. Just thought I'd let you know about some of our birds at Stalwart."

Dove Feeding

• From Ruth F. from Sault Ste. Marie: *"Here is another first, for me at least.... This afternoon I happened to notice a mourning dove sitting under a small mugho pine within 15 feet of our front window. Upon closer inspection I believe that I could see another bird deeper under the bush. It turned out that it was a baby mourning dove. The adult bird seemed to be sheltering and protecting it from me as I believe that it could see me as I them. After a couple of hours the adult was gone. Later I saw it perched in the apple tree, after a good half hour of watching for something to develop, I was rewarded to see the adult drop down to the ground, scuttle under a large spruce tree and round about make it to the baby. I could see that it was making "calls" as it was nearing the baby (throat movement). Then it began to feed by regurgitating. VERY interesting, this is at 7:15 p.m. Looking out the window now, I can see the adult but not the baby, might be tucked under "her" for the evening. As I said very interesting and I had never seen anything like that before.*

On a less happy note: some neighbor's cat, I know not whose, was in our backyard at the same time and it took a running leap at a chickadee and almost nailed it. I would have liked to dispatch the cat but didn't dare. Had a difficult time shooing it out of here because our three-year-old grandson was here and thought the cat was just the berries because it was so nice, tame and friendly. Guess that is the Nature of it all though."

Free Blue Jays

• From Ben & Debbie M. from Paradise: *"Hi Connie, we have been overwhelmed with blue jays this week, eating four gallons per day of a mixture of sunflower seeds and cracked corn. Have counted at least a hundred per attack... People are more than welcome to visit and take some jays with you... Bring your own container and ear-plugs..."*

Crow Revenge

• From James R. in Kincheloe: *"Over the weekend, I was sitting on my patio by my rock garden, listening to a flock of starlings and crows who were foraging on the grass about 75 feet away. Suddenly, a hawk came by, flying about four feet off the ground, headed for the flock.*

However, when he got there, he was met by the crows who banded togeth-er, sent up the alarm and mobbed the hawk. He quickly flew back on another course, again only 4 feet off the ground, with the crows following him about 60 feet in the air.

I never got a good look at the hawk, except to note that it was a large one. I found it unusual since the hawk passed only ten feet from my chair in my own yard.

Saw the same hawk again the next day, right here in the middle of the Kincheloe development, again being mobbed by crows. The fall migration has obviously begun."

Chickadee curiosity

I just love those little chickadees. What is it about them that is so alluring? They are bold, inquisitive and friendly at all times. They never seem to get tired and they never get discouraged. We could learn a lot from these little birds. In all my travels, I have never found anyone that did not like these little cuties.

One brisk spring day, Pat and I were sitting out on our deck eat-ing lunch and enjoying a visit from our friend Vicki. While we were sitting there, I could see chickadees buzzing all around us in the pine trees. They were busy doing who-knows-what and were bouncing and flitting through the trees. As I was eating my sand-wich, Pat said, "Don't move. You've got a chickadee sitting right next to you." Sure enough, out of the corner of my eye, I could see a tiny little bird perched on the side of the chair frame. It had a beady little eye fixed on the Cheetos on my plate! It stared at them for a long second or two, and then it took off for the safety of the pine tree again. It probably figured out that that snack was almost bigger than it was!

A few seconds later Pat said to Vicki, "Don't move, there's a bird sitting behind your head." Sure enough, a chickadee (the same one?) was precariously perched on the back of her chair and it was staring at her short hair which was gently blowing in the breeze. Vicki sat absolutely stock still and waited to see what would happen. All three of us were discussing what the bird was doing as it was intently checking out the top of her head from only a few inches away. Pat said, "I think it wants some of your hair - maybe for its nest!" Vicki said, "Well, it can have some, but I wish it would hurry up!"

After much long deliberation, the chickadee must have decided that it couldn't choose which one to take, so it flew away. We all sat and wondered about that for a few minutes. Could it be that it was already building a nest in early April? It was possible!

No matter what it was that the chickadee wanted, it was still a pleasure to be able to observe their activities from such a close distance. Birds are wonderful and I swear, they never fail to amaze me with their antics.

Birding technology

Every year, sometimes it seems like every week, new advancements in electronics grow by leaps and bounds. Even in the birding world I've been noticing changes due to the new technology. The industry has been quick to answer the needs of a fast-growing bird-feeding population.

Many bird feeders for years have been complaining about the mess associated with their hobby. Shell husks and seed casings from sunflower seed and safflower seed do leave garbage which must be cleaned up occasionally.

Not only is it a nasty sight, but quite a few of the leftover seeds also have a tendency to sprout on their own (even though the seed manufacturers claim that they bake the seed so that it won't germinate). Some seed companies are offering shelled peanuts, sunflower seed hearts, and cracked corn in bulk to meet the needs of the "tidy" bird feeder. This type of seed is especially handy if your bird feeder is mounted over a deck or porch where the debris can be dangerous to your footing.

A company called Woodinville WildBird Food offers a special blend that they call "Waste Not." It consists of sunflower chips, cracked corn, peanut chips, and niger seed. Their claim to fame is that it leaves no waste, that everything is edible except the niger hulls and they guarantee that nothing will sprout.

Sounds great, doesn't it? My only concern is that the birds will eat twice as much of it, twice as fast! It could be quite a strain on the old pocketbook. Also, one of my joys in bird feeding is watching the various kinds of birds with their unique methods of cracking open seeds.

The white-breasted nuthatches are especially thrifty some years, as I've watched them store sunflower seeds in the bark of our backyard Scotch pine trees. Are they hoarding for some awful winter weather that they can sense and we can't?

Now, just in case you know a bird lover/feeder who has everything ... birding technology has gone one step further than they have. For anyone who has ever wanted to see what goes on inside a bird house, or at the feeders while they are gone from home, Nature Vision Inc. (and many other companies now) has created a "VBS" - Video Birding Station. It is a mini audio/video camera which is mounted inside their bird-feeding station. This camera sends a signal to your TV via a microwave transmitter. You can watch bird-feeding activity from the comfort of a recliner in your own living room! Another company advertises a mini-camera as well, but it has a snake-like extender arm that can mount anywhere, from inside a bird house, to your bird feeder, to who-knows-where. Finally, the James Bond technology from the movies has made it to the birding world. Or, to quote a line from the Batman movies, "Where does he GET all those toys!?"

Pat and I were given a gift of a bird transmitter as a wedding gift many years ago and this simple gadget has delighted us and many of our house guests. It essentially is an outdoor microphone that transmits a signal to a receiver inside the house. When we turn on the receiver, the sounds from outside come blasting in - just as if you were actually standing outside.

On a cold winter day this invention is wonderful - but beware - the cold will also quickly kill the batteries that operate the transmitter and it has a short life when it's below zero degrees.

When we first installed our transmitter out into our front yard, it was a gorgeous summer day. We quickly hung it, then ran inside the house to listen to it. For a minute or two, there was only silence. Then a loud "Bzzzzzz - zzzzzzzz - zzzzzzz"ing noise followed, and the noise was QUITE loud. We looked outside to see if we could catch a glimpse of what? A hummingbird maybe? We couldn't see anything outside. Was something wrong with the transmitter?

Finally we went outside to check out the buzzing sound ... and discovered that we had been listening to a mosquito!!! Augh. Needless to say, when the birds started to come in and sing, we decided to turn down the volume a bit.

Great horned owl rescue

One afternoon I was at work when I received a phone call. "Get over to the soccer field now!" my supervisor said. I had never been to the soccer field, but I knew where it was and headed over there. Along the way, I met my supervisor, Mark. I said, "What's going on?" and he replied, "There's an owl stuck in the soccer net, we need you to help get it out." "Holy crap," I thought to myself, "How did that happen?"

We walked a bit more and came to the soccer field where there was a crowd of people gathered around one end of the field. I took a look at the net and saw a small body hopelessly entangled there. My heart sunk in my chest and I felt just awful. "Oh my God," I thought, "There's no way we can ever get that bird out alive.'" It was a medium-sized owl and it was hanging upside down with the net wrapped around one of its legs about a dozen times and the net was also entwined through a wing and around its body.

Great horned owl

Besides that, it was misting raining outside and the bird was sopping wet.

The net was so tight around its leg that I had no idea how it could ever be cut off. Two of my supervisors, Mark and Mike, were both there with me. They were all staring at the bird. I kneeled down on the wet grass to get a better look. "What do you need, Connie?" Mike asked. I told him I needed a towel, a pair of sharp scissors and a pair of very heavy-duty gloves. After taking one look at those talons, I knew my fingers were getting nowhere near the legs without a pair of gloves. Mike headed out to find the necessary items and Mark knelt on the ground with me to assess what had to be done.

I put my hand underneath the bird and lifted it a little so that it was not hanging in the net. The owl - which I now discovered was a great horned owl - snapped open its eyes and gave me a look which was very sad. It appeared to be exhausted and didn't struggle in my hand. The leg looked so terrible and painful that I used my other hand to lift it up a little so that the pressure was relieved.

Mark and I discussed how we would attempt to cut the owl free. I told him that some of the rope was too tight to cut, and that we should start with the looser ones. By now Mike had arrived

with the supplies. He handed me a pair of welder gloves - perfect for the job. Then he also handed me a pair of twine snipper-type scissors which I hoped would work.

Mark and I worked as a team, but it was hard to know where to start. I slipped one glove on and held the bird with one hand and tried to cut the ropes with the other hand. Mark pushed and pulled on the adjacent ropes to try to make them looser and easier to cut. He also put on the other glove and helped to hold the bird still.

Amazingly enough, the owl did not struggle, although I did see it close the talons on the loose leg now and then. This had to be very painful for the owl, but it did not fight our efforts. It watched us with its bright yellow eyes and would snap its beak every now and then for effect. I told Mark not to get his hand anywhere near its beak, nor the loose leg, as those talons can do some real damage on flesh.

We cut the ropes very gradually from around the leg and then were able to also cut the ropes from around the body and wing. The rope had been knotted and twisted in so many places that it had been like a jigsaw puzzle trying to figure out where to cut - especially without taking a chance on hurting the owl any more. The once-trapped leg looked terrible and I doubted that the owl was going to come away uninjured. I ran my fingers gently down the leg and couldn't feel anything unusual, so I hoped that was a good sign.

By now we had gathered quite a crowd. Mike was busy making sure that nobody got too close. We were making good progress at freeing the owl, so I asked Mike if he would get a box for me. I figured that this owl was going to have to be taken to Anne Trissell, the wildlife rehabilitator, for assessment when we were done.

As we freed the owl from the ropes, I told Mark, "Boy, we sure made a mess out of this soccer net." And he said, "That's OK. They can always buy another one." I wrapped the owl's body and legs up in the towel so that I could safely handle it without gloves and then we lifted it up so that the crowd could see that we had gotten it out of the net. There was a cheer from the people and Mark and I left the field with the owl in hand. He picked up the supplies and by now Mike had arrived with a sturdy paper box. He gave it to me and I gently put the owl, towel and all, into the box.

As I carried it away, people peppered me with questions. "What kind of owl is that?" "Where are you taking it, Miss T?" "Is that a really big owl?" "Why was it in the net?" "Is it hurt?" "Are owls good to eat?" Argh. There's always one joker in every crowd it seems.

They were all really good questions and Mark and I took a moment to answer them as best as we could. Then I begged off, saying that I had to get some professional help for the owl.

The amazing end to the story is that Anne Trissell was able to observe the owl for a few days and we came to the determination that there were no broken bones, only a few strains in its wing and leg. After a few days had passed, there were no outward signs that the owl had been injured. Its feathers dried out, it hopped and flew normally in its flight cage, and it looked like it wanted OUT of there. I went over to Anne's one day and took a look at it. The transformation was incredible. The owl was beautiful and very wild-looking.

About a week later, Anne and her husband Jerry put the owl in a carry-cage and brought it back to where I was working that day. Together Jerry and I took it close to the woods near where the soccer field was. The nervous great horned owl huddled close to the back of the cage until we opened the door. Then it

Great Horned Owl

shot out of there like a bullet and flew straight over to an oak tree, where it disappeared into its depths. Jerry and I smiled at each other and knew that our work there was done.

It only took about two or three minutes and the crows found the owl. They proceeded to caw and flap about around the tree where the owl was and become general nuisances of themselves. "Well," I thought, "Life is back to normal for the owl."

Observations

A beautiful day on the lake

• From Jim R. from Kinross: *"The wife and I went out to Bass Lake north of McMillan for a little canoeing and birding one day in October. We figured there would be some migrants coming through.*

Bass Lake is beautiful, although I am skeptical of any claim for bass. The day was still with hardly any breeze. A state forest campground is nearby, but not directly on the lake. Our Oldtown canoe was the only watercraft there that day. No cottages; the lake is completely barren of habitation except for a set of stairs and a dock that looked like they had not been used in a while.

Saw a kingfisher first, fishing from snags along the shoreline and scolding us when we interrupted him. Then we saw a diving bird that we could not immediately identify, but after research, we decided it was a red-breasted merganser. We tracked the bird along the lake as it dived and teased us until we came upon a Great Blue Heron, so we turned our attention to him and disturbed his hunting for a while. But we had heard a loon on the other side of the lake so we went there. What we found were two immature loons which did not have their full complement of mark-ings - just mainly gray and black. However, they were fishing and diving in the lake and so we tried to keep up with them. We got close a few times and heard their call. We had a good look. Enjoyable day, no bugs, no phones and enough birds to entertain."

Eagles just wanna have fun

• From Rob C.: *"Hi. I'm on Sugar Island, on the northwest side, on the river, just upriver from Lake George. There are quite a few islands out front; this morning I noticed some large birds on one of the small bare rock piles. Yep, bald eagles — two juveniles and two mature.*

The neat thing is that within a half an hour more flew in until there were a total of 9 birds! All stages of development. They were obviously 'just goofing off' — a couple would take off, wheel around and drop right in the middle of the group on the rock pile. Much wing flapping and shuffling of positions!! This went on for about an hour — finally ones and twos left till there are only 2 left now.

There are a lot of loons now — we saw a flock on the water; perhaps 16 birds. The only singles we see now are young birds.

The osprey seem to be gone — this was a good summer for them; at least we saw birds probably twice a week.

Almost time to start feeding."

Please don't sing any more

• From Jarl H., also on Sugar Island: *"One morning as I exited the house, I heard a very loud sound not unlike a thin pine board being slowly broken. I thought, 'What the —?' As I looked toward the waterfront (source), 'low-&-behold' there were two (count em) bald eagles perched side-by-side on the top of the trees and a third one speaking, flying past. All were immatures, i.e., dark body but with some speckles of white throughout. Wow! I know that the quality of my voice will not ever land me with the Metropolitan Opera, but I'm glad it's a wee bit better than that of the eagle."*

Duck Tales

• From Tom P. in Sault Ste. Marie: *"I enjoy reading your column, as always. It was especially neat to read about the tundra swans, I see several every fall while duck hunting around here, but I haven't seen a flock as big as what was spotted in Lake George recently.*

However, I have hunted for many years on the St. Clair Flats and there are hundreds if not thousands of them present there every fall. Many on Saginaw Bay, too. There are so many on Lake St. Clair, especially in St. John's Marsh, that my brother and I have gone as far as to consider making his boat-blind look like a gray cygnet, complete with long neck and head on the bow! We haven't done it yet, but he has plans drawn up.

I see lots of tundra swans in North Dakota every year, where we have hunted for them, believe it or not. Even my duck hunting buddies give me a strange look when I tell them we hunt swans (and sandhill cranes) out there. In the Dakotas, the swans are in smaller family groups and small flocks. There are many, many more on Lake St. Clair, which must be a staging area for them. I'm not sure why they can be hunted on the prairies and on the East Coast, where they winter, but not in Michigan. It could be that Michigan is off-limits since we have a growing flock of trumpeter swans, which are not legal to hunt anywhere and could easily be mistaken by the untrained eye for tundra swans.

Likewise with the sandhill cranes. As I understand it, the cranes that nest in and pass through Michigan are a subspecies that are fewer in number than the tens of thousands that pass through the Dakotas. When you go to bed at night, you can still hear cranes in your head after hearing them calling above you all day long when it's still and they're catching the thermal drafts. It is magnificent."

Tom also tells us about another neat event: *"Last year in October I shot a banded black duck in Munuscong Bay. The band was old and worn thin. There was a marked groove worn in it - even though the duck's leg showed no apparent damage - and most of the numbers were illegible. I sent the band into the Feds and they returned it in the spring after using an acid wash process to pull the numbers out. As it turns out, the duck was 13 years old! I felt terrible about shooting it after reading that.*

This year I was back in Munuscong. My dog and I were enjoying a fabulous day watching mallards move around and land within a few feet of our blind. (We try not to shoot hens, and they were the ones landing close and talking to the decoys). A black duck flew over the decoys and I shot it. When my dog brought it back to the blind, I about fell over - it was banded! You could hear the hollering across the bay.

I just received the info from the Feds on this bird. It was 1 and a half years old and was banded in Pembroke, Ontario. The old bird was banded in Harpster, Ohio. Both were drakes.

Anyway, I thought I'd share that. To shoot a banded duck is rare enough (banded geese are more common around this neck of the woods). My dad and grandfather hunted for many, many years without shooting a banded duck. The odds of shooting two banded black ducks exactly one year apart must be fairly high. I should have gone out to buy a Lotto ticket after that."

Christmas day at the Thompsons

It was Christmas day and all around the Thompson house the darkness was complete. Nothing twitched or made a move, not a mouse, a raccoon, or a bird of any sort.

Slowly, and with great deliberation, the sun gently slipped its blazing orange head up towards the horizon. As the first morning rays spilled into the yard, a scene of great beauty and serenity was revealed.

A loose coating of fluffy snow had just fallen and as the sun rose higher, each flake shone with an iridescent brilliance, each one trying to outshine the other.

Quietly and shyly, a soft "peeeeeep" was heard deep in the woods. An early bird he was, that little black-capped chickadee. He sprang from the nook where he was nestled and flew quickly to his favorite backyard perch in a bushy pine tree. From the edge of the woods came another soft cry - a rising "peeeeent!" breaking the silence. Suddenly a nuthatch fluttered in to sit next to the chickadee, then a woodpecker, then a cardinal and a goldfinch.

They all gazed in wonder at the new addition to the backyard. It was a new pine tree and ho! How it glistened and glowed in the new morning light! Where once there had been only a blank piece of lawn, now proudly stood a gaily decorated Blue Spruce tree.

The tree was strung with carefully-threaded pieces of popcorn and cranberries. Here and there, pinecones were gently hanging, heavily laden with their own peanut butter treasures. Sprinkled among the branches were also skewered small pieces of apples and oranges.

The unusual crowd of birds stared in awe and jostled one another for a better look at their Christmas present. Other birds from their families joined them and soon the trees surrounding the backyard were full of little round feathery bodies.

Then in a quick burst of speed, the chickadee, bold and full of curiosity as usual, leaped from his perch and flew over to check out one of the pinecones. A quick peck and taste revealed that indeed, this tree was no illusion. On the chickadee's heels quickly followed the finches and the nuthatches. They each sampled a few of the delicacies and proclaimed with squeeks and peeps their intense pleasure.

Finally convinced, the woodpeckers and the cardinal flew down as well. Once there, they feasted on the juicy apple pieces and delightfully sought out any chunks of crunchy peanut butter that they could find.

The birds' eyes twinkled in delight and the fluffy snow from the branches floated into the air as the jolly avians danced from branch to branch. Their joy at this unexpected discovery was apparent and soon their excited songs brought in more guests.

In came the evening and the pine grosbeaks. In came more finches - gold, purple and house finches. Skating through the snow with the greatest of ease came the ruffed grouse, and lastly, in came the king of bullies, the regal blue jay. The jay sang not a note, but went straight to his chore of wolfing down huge chunks of popcorn.

Each species of bird that came in had their own favorite foods. The chickadees, nuthatches, and woodpeckers preferred the popcorn and the peanut butter, while the grosbeaks voraciously devoured all the cranberries. The goldfinches daintily nibbled at the popcorn as well, but the cardinal preferred the apple and orange chunks, nipping off huge beakfuls and swallowing them whole.

Swimming through the snow underneath it all was the grouse, happily cleaning up any fallen debris. The myriad joyful chirps and whistles were an oasis for my household-bound ears. I leaned closer to the window to visually participate when suddenly ... all the birds in the yard froze at the sight of an intruder in the window.

Almost as one, they all opened their wings wide. Away they all flew, in the blink of an eye, chipping and chirping as they made clear their escape through the dense wood. The grouse busted out of the snow embankment where he had been feeding, and with a loud "WHIRRRRRR" sailed through the pine trees to safety.

My disappointment was extreme but I was cheered to see so many little faces peering at me from in between the snowy branches. It was possibly my imagination, but I could swear that I heard a little voice sing "Thanks for the Merry Christmas treats and we'll be back later tonight!"

Great gray owl babies

One day my friend Joe N. came to me and said, "How would you like to see some great gray owl babies? I found a nest!" 'Holy Cow!' I thought, that is a fantastic thing!

Great gray owl nests in Michigan were just about unheard of and the number that had been found can be counted on one hand. Most of the time the grays went back to their natural habitat in the more northern countries - which was Canada or the Arctic Circle. Joe had found a nest? That was truly incredible.

The summer before - exactly on the Fourth of July - Pat and I had been driving down a rural road in Chippewa County when we saw a great gray owl sitting on top of a fence post in the middle of a hayfield. We couldn't believe it - we had never seen one in Michigan in the summertime! Could this nest that Joe had found be a relative of the one we had seen the summer before?

Of course I agreed to go see it - what a great opportunity he was offering me. I had never seen baby owls - owlets - before so this would be a treat. We met at a prearranged spot early one morning at the edge of a forest and we walked through the dewy grass of the adjoining field to get to a certain spot where Joe wanted to enter the woods. Joe said, "Make sure you follow in my footsteps, we don't want to step on any of them - the owls could be anywhere."

We entered into the trees and had been walking about ten minutes when Joe pointed up. "There's where the nest is." Sure enough, a large nest made of branches was situated about 25 to 30 feet up in a leafless tree. "Now we have to find the owls," he said. We began to look around, making small circles outward from the nest tree. We searched the grasses, which were still partially flattened down from the winter and we watched where we placed our boots.

Before too long, Joe said, "There's one!" We walked up to within ten feet of an owlet sitting on the ground in the grass. "I think that's Clumsy. I've named them all so I can keep them straight," he said. The owl was keeping an eye on us, but did not seem afraid. I was intrigued - it was so very cute! It had giant, clear yellow eyes and was a large ball of gray fluff. I occupied myself with taking tons of pictures and Joe said that we could walk right up to it, that it had no fear.

However, when we got to within touching distance, the owl started to hiss at us. Joe talked to it in a calming voice and it quieted down. It had just wanted us to know that we shouldn't touch it. After a few minutes it was tired of us and started to turn and waddle through the grass away from us.

All of a sudden, BOOM! It tipped over and fell sideways into the grass. I started to chuckle, that was really cute. It laid there for a minute or two with its feet sticking in different directions and its fuzzy down all messed up. Then it reluctantly, awkwardly got to its feet, gave a squawk, and started to try to walk away again. We decided to go look for the other two chicks.

As we were searching the woods, a rustle of feathers and a soft clucking noise could be heard to one side of us. When we glanced in that direction, there was a very large great gray owl floating through the woods on silent wings. It landed about fifty feet from us. Joe said, "That's the female. She must be feeding one of the other chicks. She won't care if we go over there."

We slowly walked towards her and came around to the side so that we could see what she was doing. Mama owl had a fat mole in her beak and was trying to figure out how to give it to her chick. It was obvious that the treat was too large for the owlet standing

Clumsy

in front of her. She finally laid it on the ground, held it down with one large taloned foot and pulled it apart with her beak. Then she fed the pieces to the baby. After a few minutes, she decided she was done and took off to fly to a nearby tree to keep an eye on us.

We approached the owlet and Joe said, "That's Junior. He's the youngest one, I don't think he was ready to leave the nest yet, but they probably pushed him out." Sure enough, when we got close to Junior, I saw that he looked really tough. His fuzz was all wet in places and matted down and he had slugs crawling all over him. It made me wonder if

he had tipped over too and had laid down on the ground for way too long? The slugs disgusted Joe and he reached over to pick off as many of them as he could. We were both surprised that the

owlet didn't even seem to know that they were on him.

Junior's eyes were all red-rimmed and he looked weak and helpless. He was a direct opposite to Clumsy, who looked bright-eyed and healthy. I had a bad feeling about Junior, but was glad to see that Mom was taking good care of him. We took a few pictures, then started off looking for the third chick.

We wandered around and around, but had no luck. Joe said that

Junior

he had named the last chick Bull and that it was the largest one of the bunch. It was possible that Bull had even started to climb up on some branches or something. We just knew that we didn't have any luck looking for it on the ground and there were WAY too many trees to search them all at that time.

While we were searching, every now and then we would see Mom flying through the woods going one way or another. She continued to amaze us as she was a very large bird and she made absolutely no sound when she moved around doing her business.

Joe and I made our way out of the woods and left for the day, but not after I had thanked him profusely for allowing me to see one of the greatest wonders of the world.

Final thoughts on a new year

Whenever a new year starts, it always feels a bit daunting to me. What will the next year bring me and the rest of the world? Mankind has made huge advances in the areas of medicine, science, and industry. Even while we have done so, we have also gone backwards on the evolutionary scale by decimating whole populations of animals and birds.

Is this where man has shown his superiority and supreme intelligence? Thanks to the shortsightedness of our species, never again will any human every add a dodo from Mauritius or an elephant bird from Madagascar to his/her life lists.

The two sides of humankind are split apart.

On one hand, we have organizations such as the National Audubon Society and the Migratory Bird Conservancy which are to be commended for their strides in saving certain species of birds and encouraging others to participate in habitat restoration and preservation.

On the other hand, we have individuals who take the task upon themselves to eliminate what they consider pests. Two examples that come to mind are the nine men in New York who slaughtered hundreds of double-crested cormorants and the individual in southern Illinois who poisoned a winter wheat field, killing 27,000 migrating birds. These outbursts of violence wipe out, in a single day, the efforts of thousands of caring people who are dedicated to the preservation of life.

Hopefully, the success stories will outnumber the failures in the next year. One such success story is the peregrine falcon, whose numbers recuperated enough for it to be removed from the Endangered List in 1998. The bald eagle's numbers have also rebounded enough that it has been considered for delisting as well.

We, as birders (whose numbers are in the millions), can choose to wipe the slate clean and "make a difference" in the next year. There are many things that we can do to effect a change. An act as simple as participating in a bird count can help, or a more dedicated effort such as restoring birding habitat is always welcome.

Perhaps you could even make some New Year's Resolutions. These could include:

1. Resolve to start a new life list. Label this one your "New Century List."

2. Resolve to get at least one non-birder interested in watching birds. This could be anyone from a neighbor and a friend to a relative. Maybe you could play on their competitive spirit and make a game or a wager out of it?

3. Resolve to fill your bird feeders more regularly and to clean them once a month. Also try to provide fresh water for the birds at all times. Putting it on your list of things "to do" once a week really helps.

4. Resolve to read bird magazines in public to increase avian awareness. Perhaps subscribe to a birding magazine, then when you are finished with it, discreetly leave it in the waiting room at your doctor or dentist's office.

5. Resolve to replace any of your birding equipment that is worn or over-used with newer equipment. There are many wonderful new binoculars and scopes that offer incredible views like never before - and in all price ranges.

6. Resolve to make every bird experience a fun one and to look at the birds with new eyes. Don't just identify them, but observe how they live, how they interact and how they cherish each moment as if it could be their last.

7. Resolve to approach every birding encounter with wonder. Try to notice something new about every bird you see - even the ones that you have seen hundreds of times before.

Birds are everywhere in our lives, and they can be a constant source of delight. Take a second today to slow down and really look with your eyes wide open. Our lives pass in the blink of an eye and it is up to you to make every moment count - Good birding everyone!

PHOTOGRAPHY CREDITS

*(all photographs were taken by Connie M. Thompson,
unless otherwise noted below)*

1   Common Loon in St. Marys River near the Soo Locks Boat Tours Dock in Sault Ste. Marie, Michigan, 2010

5   "Fake" bald eagle nest with bald eagle sitting on edge, constructed on top of a tall tower near the town of Strongs, 2003

7   Sandhill crane flying over grassy field near the woods on Ridge Road, Barbeau, 2001

12   Bald eagle sitting in tree on 15 Mile Road, Barbeau, 2002

13   Mute swan walking across snow and sand to chase us off at Traverse City waterfront, 1994

15   Pileated woodpecker on bird feeder on Sugar Island: photo courtesy of Jarl Hiltunen, 1999

17   Juvenile Cooper's Hawk being held in the hand of a bird bander at Whitefish Point Bird Observatory, 2003

21   Great gray owl sitting in a willow tree in our front yard, Barbeau, 1998

23   Sharptail grouse feeding in yard in Pickford: photo courtesy of Howard Anderson, 1998

23   Red-breasted nuthatch on hand on Sugar Island: photo courtesy of Jarl Hiltunen, 1999

23   Yellow birch tree on Sugar Island with knots in bark resembling eyes: photo courtesy of Jarl Hiltunen, 1999

27   Common Raven, body found in snow in the back of our property, 2011

31   Blue jay on bird feeder in our backyard: photo courtesy of Patsy Newman, 2010

34   Pat Thompson and Larry Dech in our driveway on a snowy winter's day, 1999

38   Bald eagles feeding on carcass: photo courtesy of Joe Nault, 2004

through it on a cold winter's evening, 2001

213   Great horned owl caught in soccer net: photo taken by
Cathy Cryderman, 2010

214   Great horned owl leg with soccer net wrapped around it:
photo taken by Cathy Cryderman, 2010

216   Great horned owl sitting in flight cage recuperating at Anne
Trissell's house, 2010

223   Clumsy, a great gray owlet, 2010

224   Junior, a great gray owlet shortly after it came out of the
nest, 2010

224   Junior, a great gray owlet that has now started to climb
trees, 2010

225   Junior, a great gray owlet that is now just about ready to fly,
2010

Front Cover

- Clumsy, a great gray owlet, photo taken in grassy area near
nest site in Barbeau, MI, 2010

Back Cover

- Two juvenile pileated woodpeckers playing a game of tag
on the roadside on M-129, just north of Cedarville, MI,
2010

- A sharp-tailed grouse dashing into the weeds on Riverside
Drive, Barbeau, MI, 2010

Connie M. Thompson

Connie M. Thompson has been writing about birds since 1999. In that time she has written over 280 articles for *The Evening News* based in Sault Ste. Marie, Michigan. After 2005, she discontinued writing for the newspaper and continued writing about birds and their antics in a monthly 4-page full-color newsletter called *Birds In Our Backyards*.

The newsletter includes updates on new birding products, local bird sightings, stories, and occasional guest writers who share their own specialties. Feature stories include a Reader's Spotlight where Connie highlights beautiful photographs taken by readers and a monthly photography tips column. There are also bird feeding tips and poetry in the newsletter. A popular portion continues to be the bird sightings from all over the state. People comment that it is their favorite part of the newsletter, as it allows them to know what birds their neighbors are seeing and what they too can expect to see.

Connie continues to offer the e-mailed version of the newsletter free to an extensive list of bird-lovers around the country. If you would like to have your name added to the list, just drop her an e-mail at bbirder@hughes.net. For those that would rather use snail mail, a subscription to the newsletter is available at an annual cost of just $18.

Connie is also an award-winning feature writer and photographer for the *UP Magazine/Porcupine Press Publications* based in Chatham, Michigan. Since 2004, she has written over 250 articles about interesting people, places and events in Michigan. She has interviewed fur trappers, barnwood builders, basket and knife makers, authors, jewelers, and everyone in between.

Connie and her husband Pat have also owned and operated their own home-based craft business since 1994. For many years they offered hand-made and hand-painted bird feeders, butterfly houses, bat houses, squirrel feeders, walking sticks, and a limited line of bird houses available for sale at hundreds of craft shows around the state of Michigan.

During their active years from 1995 to 2006, the Thompsons made and sold over 22,000 bird feeders (8 different kinds) country-wide.

In addition to that, they sold almost 300 walking sticks, 350 butterfly houses, 500 bat houses, and over 980 squirrel feeders.

The Thompson's most popular feeder was their fruit/suet feeder *(shown here)*. For the past 17 years, Pat has drilled a staggering number of four-inch holes for these fruit feeders to accommodate an orange or a grapefruit to bring in the beautiful orioles, sapsuckers, catbirds, hummingbirds and grosbeaks. All in all, almost 9,000 of these have been sold.

One of the Thompson's large 20-inch painted bird feeders *(see photo next page)* was featured on the cover of *Birds and Blooms* magazine in December 1999, and a feature story inside the issue detailed how they are able to make and sell so many gorgeous cedar bird feeders.

The smaller version of the featured bird feeder (what they call a 12-inch) was one of the most popular sellers

and over 2,400 of the feeders shown here currently reside at homes in Michigan.

Pat and Connie are still busy in their workshop and art studio making bird feeders and various other craft items. Connie is involved in making some new prototypes - which will be tested in their backyard as always. Thousands of birds have tried out their bird feeders before a single one is ever sold to the public.

Today their bird feeders are sold only in limited numbers and a small part of their product line can be found online at www.etsy.com/shop/CedarBreezes.

The Thompsons would love to hear from you about your own experiences with feathered friends. You can either write to them at 14488 S. Ridge Rd., Dafter, MI 49724 or send an e-mail to: bbirder@hughes.net.

ORDER FORM

Book:	Price	Qty.	Total
A Fascination for Feathers	$15.50		
	Subtotal		
	Tax *(MI residents 6%)*		
	Shipping & Handling *(see below for quantity pricing)*		
	TOTAL		

Please add the following shipping and handling charges:
1-2 books - $4.00
3-4 books - $6.00
5+ books - $8.00

SHIP TO:

Name _____

Address _____

City _____ State ____ Zip _____

Phone (_____) _____

❏ Visa   ❏ Mastercard   ❏ Discover   ❏ Check/Money Order
(payable in U.S. Funds)

Card Number _____

Expiration Date _____

Signature _____

PLEASE MAIL TO:

RIDGE ROAD ENTERPRISES
14488 S. Ridge Road, Dafter, MI 49724
or call (906) 635-5336 or email: bbirder@hughes.net

INDEX

BOLD page numbers indicate photographs

Common Redpolls fighting over some seeds that they found in a melted snowman.

Blue Jays will assume any pose at all when in pursuit of the very last peanut.

This immature snowy owl was oblivious to any photographers as it
scanned the snowy fields for dinner.

All black and white graphics illustrated by Connie M. Thompson
©2011

Made in the USA
Lexington, KY
31 July 2012